THE MYSTERY OF THE TRINITY

The Mystery of the Trinity

Mission of the Spirit

8 lectures in Dornach, Oxford, and London
July and August 1922
(CW 214)

Rudolf Steiner

This edition copyright © 2016 SteinerBooks
An imprint of Anthroposophic Press, Inc.
610 Main Street, Great Barrington, MA 01230
www.SteinerBooks.org

All rights reserved. No part of this book may be reproduced in any form without the written permission of the publisher, except for brief quotation embodied in critical reviews and articles. This work is a translation of lectures 1 to 4 and 8 to 11 of *Das Geheimnis der Trinität: Der Mensch und sein Verhältnis zur Geisteswelt im Wandel der Zeiten* (vol. 214 of the Collected Works [CW] of Rudolf Steiner) published in German by Rudolf Steiner Verlag, Dornach, Switzerland.

Translation by James H. Hindes
Revised for this updated 2nd edition

Cover Image: *Holy Trinity,* fresco (1739)
by Luca Rossetti da Orta (1708–1770)
(San Gaudenzio, Ivrea, Italy).
Cover and book design by Jens Jensen

LIBRARY OF CONGRESS CONTROL NUMBER: 2016913629

ISBN: 978-162148-095-2 (paperback)
ISBN: 978-162148-096-9 (eBook)

Contents

PART ONE: THE MYSTERY OF THE TRINITY

    Lecture One   9

    Lecture Two   29

    Lecture Three   43

    Lecture Four   59

PART TWO: THE MISSION OF SPIRIT

    Meditation: The Path to Higher Knowledge   77

    The Cosmic Origin of the Human Form   98

    The Mystery of Golgotha   115

    The Other Side of Human Existence   131

Notes   157

Part One

The Mystery of the Trinity

Lecture One

Dornach, July 23, 1922

We have pointed out that the spiritual life of the first four centuries of Christianity has been completely buried, that everything written today about the views and knowledge of human beings living at the time of The Mystery of Golgotha and during the four centuries thereafter is based on sources that have come to us essentially through the writings of the opponents of gnosticism. This means that the "backward seeing" of the spiritual researcher is necessary to create a more exact picture of what actually took place during these first four Christian centuries. In this sense I have recently attempted to present a picture of Julian the Apostate.[1]

Now, we cannot say that the following centuries, as presented in the usual historical descriptions, are very clear to people today. What we could call the soul life of the European population from the fifth on into the twelfth, thirteenth, and fourteenth centuries remains completely unclear in the usual historical portrayals. What do we find, then, basically represented in these usual historical portrayals? And what do we find even if we look at the writings of facile, so-called dramatists and authors, writers such as Ernst von Wildenbruch,[2] whose writings are, in essence, nothing more than the family histories of Louis the Pious or other similar personages, garnished with superficial pageantry, and then presented to us as history?

It is extremely important to look at the truth concerning European life during those times when so much of the present originated. If we want to understand anything at all concerning the deeper streams of culture, including the culture of recent times, we must understand the soul life of the European population in those times.

Here I would like to begin with something that will, no doubt, be somewhat remote from many of you; we need, however, to address this subject because it can only be seen properly today in the light of spiritual science. As you know there is something today called "theology." This theology—basically all of today's European theology—actually came into being in its fundamental structure and inner nature during the fourth and fifth centuries after Christ and through the following very dark centuries up to the twelfth and thirteenth centuries, when it was brought to a certain conclusion through Scholasticism. From the view of this theology, which was really developed only in its basic nature in the time after Augustine, who himself could no longer be understood—or, at best, he could be barely understood. However, all that preceded him—for example, what was said about The Mystery of Golgotha—could no longer be understood at all.[3]

Let's consider the essence of this theology that developed precisely during the darkest times of the Middle Ages, darkest, that is, for our external knowledge. Above all, it becomes clear to us that this theology is something entirely different from the theology that came before it—if indeed what came before can be called theology. What theology had been before was actually only transplanted like a legacy into the times when the theology I just described arose. And you can get an impression of what earlier theology was like if you read the short essay on Dionysius the Areopagite in this week's edition of the *Goetheanum*.[4] There you will find a portrayal of the way human beings related to the world in the first Christian centuries, a way altogether different from what came to prevail by the time of the ninth, tenth, and following centuries.

In contrast to the later, newer theology, the old theology—the theology that produced Dionysius the Areopagite—saw everything that related to the spiritual world from *within* and had a direct view of what happens in the spiritual worlds. If we want to gain insight into the way adherents of this old theology actually thought, into the way the soul of this theology inwardly regarded things, then once again we can really only do so with the methods of present-day anthroposophic spiritual science.

We then come to the following results. (Yesterday, from another point of view I characterized something very similar.)[5]

In the ascent to Imagination, in the entire process of climbing, ascending to imaginative knowledge, we notice more and more that we are dwelling suspended in spiritual processes. This "hovering" in spiritual processes with our entire soul life we experience as if we were coming into contact with beings who do not live on the physical plane. Perceptions from our sense organs cease, and we experience that, to a certain extent, everything that is sense perception disappears. But during the whole process it seems as if we were being helped by beings from a higher world. We come to understand these as the same beings that the old theology had beheld as *angels, archangels*, and *archai*. I could, therefore, say that the angels help us to penetrate up into imaginative knowledge. The sensory world "breaks up," just as clouds disperse, and we see into what is behind the sensory world. Behind the sensory world a capacity that we can call Inspiration opens up; behind this sensory world is then revealed the second hierarchy, the hierarchy of the *exusiai, dynamis*, and *kyriotetes*. These ordering and creative beings present themselves to the inspired knowledge of the soul. And when we ascend further still, from Inspiration to Intuition, then we come to the first hierarchy, the *thrones, cherubim,* and *seraphim.* Through immediate spiritual training we can experience the realities that the older theologians actually referred to when they used such terms as first, second, and third hierarchy.

Now, it is just when we look at the theology of the first Christian centuries, which has been almost entirely stamped out, that we notice the following: in a certain way that early theology still had an awareness that when humanity directs its senses toward the ordinary, sensory, external world, people may see the phenomena of that world and may believe in their existence, but they do not actually know that world. There is a very specific consciousness present in this old theology—consciousness that one must first have experienced something in the spiritual world before the concepts present themselves with which one can then approach the sensory world and, as it were, illuminate it with ideas gained from the spiritual world.

In a certain way this also corresponds to the views resulting from an older, dreamlike, atavistic clairvoyance, under the influence of which people first looked into a spiritual world—though only with dreamlike perceptions—and then applied what they experienced there to their sense perceptions. If it had happened that these people had only a view of the sensory world before them, it would have seemed to them as if they were standing in a dark room with no light. However, if they first had their spiritual vision, a result of pure seeing into the world of the spirit, and then applied it to the sensory world—if, for example, they had first beheld something of the creative powers of the animal world and then applied that vision to the outer, physical animals—then they would feel as though they were walking into the dark room with a lamp. They would feel that they were walking into the world of the senses and illuminating it with a spiritual mode of viewing. Only in this way was the sensory world truly known.

This was the consciousness of these older theologians. For this reason the entire Christology of the first Christian centuries was actually viewed *from within*. The process that took place, the descent of Christ into the earthly world, was essentially seen not from the outside but rather from the inside, from the spiritual side. One first sought out Christ in spiritual worlds and then followed him as he descended into the physical, sensible world. That was the consciousness of the older theologians.

Then the following happened: the Roman world, which the Christian impulse followed in its greatest westward development, was permeated in its spiritual understanding with an inclination, a fondness, for the abstract. The Romans tended to translate perceptions, observations, and insights into abstract concepts. However, the Roman world was actually decaying and falling apart while Christianity gradually spread toward the west. And, in addition, the northern peoples were pushing from the eastern part of Europe into the west and the south. Now, it is remarkable that at the very time Rome was decaying and the fresh peoples from the north were arriving, a college was created on the Italian peninsula, a collegium that I spoke of recently that set itself the task of using all these events to completely root out the old views and modes of seeing, to allow to survive for posterity only those writings with which this college felt comfortable.[6]

History reports nothing concerning these events; nevertheless, they were real. If such a history did exist, it would point out how this college was created as a successor to the pontifical college of ancient Rome. Everything that this college did not allow was thoroughly swept away and what remained was modified before being passed on to posterity. Just as Rome invented the last will and testament as a part of its national economic order so that the dispositions of the individual human will could continue to work beyond the individual's life, so there arose in this college the desire to have the essence of Rome live on in the following ages of historical development if only as an inheritance, as the mere sum of dogmas that had been developed over many generations. "For as long as possible nothing new shall be seen in the spiritual world"—so decreed this college. "The principle of initiation shall be completely rooted out and destroyed. Only the writings we are now modifying are to survive for posterity." If the facts were to be presented in a dry, objective fashion they would be presented in this way. Entirely different destinies would have befallen Christianity—it would have been entirely rigidified—had not the northern peoples come pushing into the west and the south. These northern peoples brought with them their own natural talent, a predisposition entirely different from that of the southern peoples, the Greeks and the Romans—different, that is, from that earlier southern predisposition that had originated the older theology.

In earlier times at least, the talent of the southern peoples had been the following. Among the earlier Romans, and even more among the earlier Greeks, there were always individuals from the mass of the people who developed themselves and passed through an initiation and then could see into the spiritual world. The older theology arose with this vision, theology that possessed a direct perception of the spiritual world. Such vision in its last phase is preserved in the theology of Dionysius the Areopagite. Let us consider one of the older theologians, say from the first or second century after The Mystery of Golgotha—one of those theologians who still drew wisdom from the old science of initiation. If he had wanted to present the essence, I would like to say, the principles of his theology, he would have said, *To have any relationship to the spiritual world, human beings must first obtain knowledge of the spiritual world, either directly through their own initiation or pupils of an initiate.* After acquiring ideas and concepts in the spiritual world, they could apply those ideas and concepts to the world of the senses. Those were more or less the abstract principles of such an older theologian. The whole tendency of the older theological mood predisposed the soul to see the events in the world *inwardly:* first to see the spiritual and then to admit to oneself that the sensible world can be seen only if one starts from the spiritual. Such theology could result only as the ripest product of an old atavistic clairvoyance, for atavistic clairvoyance was also an inner seeing or perception, though only of dreamlike imaginations.

First, the peoples coming from the north had nothing of this older theological drive, which, as I said, was so strong in the Greeks. The natural abilities of the Gothic peoples, the Germanic, did not allow such a theological mood to rise up directly in the soul in an unmediated way. To properly understand the drive that these northern peoples brought into the development of Europe in the following ages (through the Germanic tribes, the Goths, the Anglo-Saxons, the Franks, and so on) we must resort to spiritual scientific means, for recorded history reports nothing of this. Initiates, able to see directly into the spiritual world to survey from that vantage point the sensory world, could not arise from within the ranks of these peoples storming down from the north because their inner soul disposition was different. These peoples were themselves still somewhat atavistically clairvoyant; they were actually still at an earlier, more primitive stage of humanity's development. These peoples—Goths, Lombards, and so on—still brought some of the old clairvoyance with them. But this old clairvoyance was not related to *inner* perceptions— to spiritual perceptions, yes—but rather to spiritual perceptions of things *outer*. The northern peoples did not see the spiritual world from the *inside*, so to speak, as had the southern peoples. The Northerners saw the spiritual world from the *outside*.

What does it mean to say that these peoples saw the spiritual world from the *outside*? Say that these people saw a brave man die in battle. The life in which they saw this man spiritually from the *outside* was not at an end for them. Now, with his death, they could follow him—still from the *outside* spiritually speaking—on his path into the spiritual world. They could follow not only the way this man lived into the spiritual world but also the ways he continued to be active on behalf of human beings on the Earth. And so these northern peoples could say: Someone or other has died, after this or that significant deed, perhaps, or after his having been the leader of this people or that tribe. We see his soul, how it continues to live, how (if he had been a soldier) he is received by the great soldiers in Valhalla, or how he lives on in some other way. This soul, this man, is still here. He continues to live and is actually present. Death is merely an event that takes place here on the Earth. Such an experience, having come with the northern peoples, was present in the fourth and fifth on through the twelfth and thirteenth centuries before being essentially buried. This was the perception of the dead as actually always present, the awareness that the souls of human beings who were greatly venerated were still present, even for earthly human beings. They were even still able to lead in battle. People of that time thought of these souls as still present and not disappearing from the earthly. With the forces given them by the spiritual world these souls continued, in a certain sense, the functions of their earthly lives. The atavistic clairvoyance of the northern peoples was such then, that, as they saw the activities of people here on Earth, they also beheld a kind of shadow world directly above people on Earth. The dead were in this shadow world. One needed only to look—these people felt—to see that those from the last and next to last generation actually continue to live. They are here; we experience community with them. For them to be present we need only to listen up into their realm.

This feeling, that the dead are here, was present, was incredibly strong, in the time that followed the fourth century, when the northern culture mixed with the Roman. You see, the northern peoples took Christ into this way of perceiving. They looked first at this world of the dead, who were actually the truly living. They saw hovering above them entire populations of the dead, and they beheld these dead as being actually more alive than themselves. They did not seek Christ here on the Earth among people walking in the physical world; they sought Christ there where these living dead were. There they sought him as one who is really present above the Earth. And you will only get the proper feeling concerning the *Heliand*, which was supposedly written by a Saxon priest, if you develop these ways of perceiving.[7] The descriptions in the *Heliand* follow these old German customs. You will understand the *Heliand's* concrete description of Christ among living human beings only if you understand that actually the scenes are to be transplanted half into the kingdom of shadows where the living dead are dwelling. You will understand much more, if you truly grasp this predisposition, this ability, which came about through the mixing of the northern with the Roman peoples.

There is something recorded in literary history to which people should actually give a great deal of thought. However, people of the present age have almost entirely given up the ability to think about such clearly startling phenomena found in the life of humanity. But pursuing literary history, you will find, for example, writings in which Charlemagne (742–814) is mentioned as a leader in the Crusades. Charlemagne is simply listed as a leader in the Crusades.[8] Indeed, you will find Charlemagne described as a living person again and again throughout the entire time that followed the ninth century. People everywhere called upon him. He is described as if he were there. When the Crusades began, centuries after his death, poems were written describing Charlemagne as if he were with the crusaders marching against the infidels.

We only understand such writings properly if we know that in the so-called dark centuries of the Middle Ages, the true history of which is entirely obliterated, there was this awareness of the living multitudes of the dead, who lived on as shadows. It was only later that Charlemagne was placed in the Untersberg. Much later, when the spirit of intellectualism had grown strong enough for this life in the shadows to have ceased, then Charlemagne was transplanted into the Untersberg (and, as another example, Frederick Barbarossa, the Holy Roman Emperor, into Kyffhaeuserberg).[9] Until that time people knew that Charlemagne was still living among them.

But wherein did these people, who atavistically saw the dead living above them, wherein did these people seek their Christianity, their Christology, their Christian way of seeing? They sought it in this way: they directed their sight toward what results when a living dead person like Charlemagne, who was revered in life, came before their souls with all those who were still his followers. And so through long ages Charlemagne was seen undertaking the first crusade against the infidels in Spain. But he was seen in such a way that the entire crusade was actually transplanted into the shadow world. The people of that time saw this crusade in the shadow world after it had been undertaken on the physical plane; they let it continue working in the shadow world—as an image of the Christ who works in the world. Therefore, Christ was described riding south toward Spain among the twelve paladins, one of whom was a Judas who eventually betrayed the entire endeavor.[10] So we see how clairvoyant perception was directed toward the *outside* of the spiritual world—not, as in earlier times, toward the *inside*—but rather

Lecture One

now toward the outside, toward what results when one looks at the spirits from the outside just as one looked at them earlier from the inside. Now, the splendor of the Christ event was reflected onto all the most important things that took place in the world of shadows.

From the fourth to the thirteenth and fourteenth centuries there lived in Europe the idea that people who had died, if they had accomplished important deeds in life, arranged their afterlife so as to enable themselves to be seen with something like a reflected splendor, an image, of the Christ event. One saw everywhere the continuation of the Christ event—if I may express myself so—as shadows in the air. If people had spoken of the things they felt, they would have said: Above us the Christ stream still hovers; Charlemagne undertook to place himself in this Christ stream and with his paladins he created an image of Christ with the twelve apostles; the deeds of Christ were continued by Charlemagne in the true spiritual world.

This was how people thought of these things in the so-called dark time of the Middle Ages. There was the spiritual world, seen from without, I would like to say, as if imaged after the sensory world, like a shadow picture of the sensory world (whereas in the earlier times, of which the old theology was only a weak reflection, the spiritual world was seen from within). For merely intellectual human beings the difference between this physical world and the spiritual world is such that an abyss exists between the two. This difference did not exist in the first centuries of the Middle Ages, in the so-called Dark Ages. The dead remained with the living. During the first period after their death, after they had been born into the spiritual world, especially outstanding and revered personalities underwent a novitiate to become saints.

For the people of those times to speak of these living dead as if they were real personalities after they had been born into the spiritual world—this was not unusual. And you see, a number of these living dead, especially chosen ones, were called to become guardians of the Holy Grail. Specially chosen living dead were designated as guardians of the Holy Grail. And the Grail legend could never be completely understood without the knowledge of who these guardians of the Grail actually were. To say: "Then the guardians of the Grail weren't real people" would have seemed laughable to the people of that time. For they would have said: Do you who are only shadow figures walking on the Earth really believe that you are more real than those who have died and now are gathered around the Grail? To those who lived in those times it would have appeared laughable for the little figures here on the Earth to consider themselves more real than the living dead. We must feel our way into the souls of that time, and this is simply how those souls felt. Their consciousness of this connection with the spiritual world meant much for the world, and much for their souls. They would have said to themselves: To begin with, the people here on the Earth consist of nothing more than what they are, right now, directly here. However, humans of the present will become proper and good only if they take into themselves what one of the living dead can give them.

In a certain sense, physical human beings on the Earth were seen as though they were merely vehicles for the outer working of the living dead. It was a peculiarity of those centuries that one said, *If the living dead want to accomplish something for which hands are needed here on Earth, then they enter a physically incarnated human being and do it through that one.* Not only that, but there were, furthermore, people in those times who said to themselves: *One can do no better than to provide a vehicle for human beings who were revered while living on the Earth and who have now become beings of such importance in the realm of the living dead that it is granted to them to guard the Holy*

Grail. The view existed among the people of those times that individuals could dedicate themselves to the Order of the Swan. Such people dedicated themselves to the Order of the Swan who wanted the knights of the Grail to be able to work through them here in the physical world. Those through whom knights of the Grail worked here in the physical world were called Swans.

Now consider the Lohengrin legend.[11] When Elsa of Brabant is in great need, the swan comes. The swan who appears is a member of the Knights of the Swan, who has received into himself a companion of the circle of the Holy Grail. One is not permitted to ask him about his secret. In that century, and also in the following centuries, princes such as Henry I of Saxony were happiest of all when, as in his campaign into Hungary, he was able to have this Knight of the Swan, this Lohengrin, in his army.[12]

But there were knights of many kinds who regarded themselves primarily as only outer vehicles for those from the other side of death who were still fighting in the armies. They wanted to be united with the dead; they knew they were united with them. The legend has actually become quite abstract today. We can only evaluate its significance for the living if we live into the soul life of the people alive at that time. And this understanding, which first looks simply and solely upon the physical world and sees how the spiritual humankind arises from the physical human and afterward belongs to the living dead, this understanding ruled the hearts and minds of that time and was the most essential element in their souls. They felt that one must first have known a human being on the Earth, that only then can one rise to that spirit. In fact, the whole understanding was reversed, even in the popular concepts of the masses in contrast to the older views. In ancient times, people had looked first into the spiritual world; they strove, if possible, to see humans as spiritual beings before their descent to Earth. Then, it was said, one can understand what the human being is on Earth. But now, the following idea emerged among these northern peoples, after they had mixed with Roman civilization: *We understand the spiritual if we have first followed it in the physical world and it has then lifted itself out of the physical world as spiritual.* This was the reverse of what had prevailed before.

The reflected splendor of this view then became the theology of the Middle Ages. The old theologians had said: *First one must have the ideas, first one must know the spiritual.* The concept of faith would have been something entirely absurd for these old theologians, for they first recognized the spiritual before they could even begin to think of knowing the physical, which had to be illumined by the spiritual. Now, however, when in the world at large people were starting from the point of view of knowing the physical, it came to this, even in theology. Theologians began to think in this way: *For knowledge, one must start with the world of senses. Then, from things of the senses one must extract the concepts—no longer bring the concepts from the spiritual world to the things of sense, but now extract the concepts from the things of sense themselves.*

Now imagine the Roman world in its decline; then imagine, within that world, what still remained as a struggle from the ancient time: namely, the fact that concepts were experienced in the spiritual world and then brought to meet the things of the senses. This was felt by such a man as Martianus Capella, who in the fifth century wrote his treatise, *De Nuptiis Philologiae et Mercurii*, wherein he wrestled still to find within the spiritual world itself what was becoming increasingly abstract in the life of ideas.[13] But this old view went under because the Roman conspiracy against the spirit—in that college or committee I have told you about—had destroyed everything representing a direct

Lecture One

human connection with the spirit. We see how that direct connection gradually vanished. The old vision ceased. Living in the old conception a human being knew: *When I reach over into the spiritual world angels accompany me.* If they were Greeks they called them "guardians." Those who went forth on the path of the spirit knew they were accompanied by a guardian spirit.

What in ancient times had been a real spiritual being, the guardian, was *grammatica*, the first stage of the seven liberal arts, at the time when Capella wrote. In ancient times, people had known that what lives in grammar, in words and syntax, can lead up into Imagination. They knew that the angel, the guardian, was working in the relationships between words. If we read the old descriptions, nowhere would we ever find an abstract definition. It is interesting that Capella does not describe grammar as the later Renaissance did. To him grammar is still a real person. So, too, rhetoric at the second stage is still a real person. For the later Renaissance such figures became mere allegories—straw figures for intellectual concepts. In earlier times they had also been spiritual perceptions that did not merely edify as they did in Capella's writings. They had been creative beings, and the entry that they had initiated into the spirit was felt as a penetration into a realm of creative beings. Now with Capella they had become allegories; but nevertheless, at least they were still allegorical. Though they were no longer stately, though they had become very pale and thin, they were still ladies: *grammatica, rhetorica, dialectica.* They were very thin and weak. All that was left of them, as it were, was the bones of spiritual effort and the skin of concepts; nevertheless, they were still quite respectable ladies who carried Capella, the earliest to write on the seven liberal arts, into the spiritual world. One by one he made the acquaintance of these seven ladies: first the lady *grammatica,* then the lady *rhetorica,* the lady *dialectica,* the lady *arithmetica,* the lady *geometria*, the lady *musica*, and finally the heavenly lady *astrologia*, who towered over them all. These were certainly ladies, and as I said, there were seven of them. The sevenfold feminine leads us onward and upward, so might Capella have concluded when describing his path to wisdom. But think of what became of it in the monastery schools of the later Middle Ages. When these later writers labored at grammar and rhetoric they no longer felt that "the eternal feminine leads us onward and upward." And that is really what happened: Out of the living being there first came the allegorical and then the merely intellectual abstraction.

Homer, who in ancient times had sought the way from the humanly spoken word to the cosmic word so that the cosmic word might pass through him, had to say, "Sing me, O muse, of Peleus' son, Achilles." From the stage when a spiritual being led persons on to the point in the spiritual world where it was no longer they themselves but the muse who sang of the wrath of Achilles—from that stage to the stage when rhetoric herself was speaking in the Roman way, and then to the mingling of the Roman with the life that came down from the north—was a very long way. Finally, everything became abstract, conceptual, and intellectual. The farther we go toward the east and into ancient times the more we find everything immersed in concrete spiritual life; theologians of old had gone to the spiritual beings for their concepts, which they then applied to this world. But theologians who grew from what arose from the merger of the northern peoples with the Roman said: *Knowledge must be sought here in the sensory world; here we gain our concepts.* But they could not rise into the spiritual world with those concepts. The Roman college had thoroughly seen to it that although people might angle around down here in the world of senses, they could not get beyond this world. Formerly, people had also had the world of the senses, but they had sought and found their concepts and ideas in the spiritual world; such concepts then helped them to illumine the physical world. Now, however, they extracted their concepts from the physical world itself, and they did not get far but reached only an interpretation of the physical world. They could no longer reach upward by an independent path of knowledge. Nonetheless, they still had a legacy from the past. It was written down or preserved in traditions embodied in and rigidified by dogmas; it was preserved in the creed. Whatever could be said about the spirit was contained therein. It was there. They increasingly reached a kind of consciousness whereby all that had been said about the realms above as a result of higher revelation must remain untouched. Revelations could no longer be checked. The kind of knowledge that can be checked now remained below; our conceptual life must now be obtained here in the physical world.

So in the course of time what had still been present in the first dark centuries of the Middle Ages persisted merely as a written legacy. It had become quite another time, when the medieval, atavistic clairvoyance of the Saxon "peasant" (as he was called—though, as the *Heliand* shows they were, in any case, priests born of the peasantry) still existed in Europe. Simply looking at the human beings around him, the Saxon peasant-priest had the faculty to see how the soul and spirit goes forth at death and becomes the dead and yet alive, living human being. Thus, in the train of those that hover over the earthly realm, he describes his vision of the Christ event in the poem, the *Heliand*.

But what was living here on the Earth was drawn further and further down into the realm of the merely lifeless. Atavistic clairvoyant abilities came to an end, and people now only sought for concepts in the sensory world. What kind of a view and attitude resulted? It was this: There is no need to pay heed to the suprasensory when it comes to knowledge. What we need is contained in the sacred writings and traditions. We need refer only to the old books and look into the old traditions. Everything we should know about the suprasensory is contained there. And now in the environment of the sensory world, we are not confused if for knowledge we take into account only the concepts contained in the sensory world itself.

More and more this consciousness came to life; the suprasensory is preserved for us and will so remain. If we want to do research we must limit ourselves to the sensory world. Someone who remained entirely within this habit of mind, who continued, as it were, in the nineteenth century this activity of extracting concepts out of the sensory world that the Saxon peasant-priest who wrote the *Heliand* had practiced, was Gregor Mendel.[14] Why should we concern ourselves with investigations of the ancient times into matters of heredity? They are all recorded in the Old Testament. Let us look, rather, down into the world of sense and see how the red and the white sweet peas will cross with one another, giving rise to red, white, and speckled flowers and so forth. Thus you can become a mighty scientist without coming into conflict or disharmony with what is said about the suprasensory, which remains untouched. It was precisely our modern theology, evolved out of the old theology along the lines I have characterized, that impelled people to investigate nature in the manner of Gregor Mendel, whose approach was that of a genuine Catholic priest.

And then what happened? Natural scientists, whose science is so "free from bias," subsequently canonized Gregor Mendel as a saint. Although this is not their way of speaking, we can describe Mendel's fate in these terms. At first they treated him without respect; now they canonize him after their fashion, proclaiming him a great scientist in all their academies. All this is not without its inner connections. The science of the present time is only possible inasmuch as it is constituted in such a way as to regard as a great scientist precisely one who stands so thoroughly upon the standpoint of medieval theology! The natural science of our time is through and through the continuation of the essence of Scholastic theology—its subsequent proliferation, its diversification. It is the continuation into our time of the Scholastic era. Hence it is quite proper for Johann Gregor Mendel to be subsequently recognized as a great scientist; that he is, but in the good Catholic sense. It made good Catholic sense for Mendel to look only at sweet peas as they cross with one another, it was following Catholic principle, because all that is suprasensory is contained in the sacred traditions and books. But we see that this does not make sense for natural scientists, none in the least—only if they are bent on stopping short at the stage of ignoramuses and giving themselves up to complete agnosticism would it make any sense to limit research to the sensory world.

This is the fundamental contradiction of our time. This contradiction is what we must be attentive to. For if we fail to look at these spiritual realities we shall never understand the source of all the confusion, of all the contradictions and inconsistencies, in the endeavors of the present day. But the easygoing comfort of our time does not allow people to awaken and really to look into these contradictory tendencies.

Think what will happen when all that is said about today's world events becomes history. Posterity will get this history. Do you think they will get much truth? Certainly not. Yet history for us has been made in this very way. These puppets of history, which are described in the usual textbooks, do not represent what has really happened in human evolution. We have arrived at a time when it is absolutely necessary for people to learn to know what the real events are. It is not enough for all the legends to be recorded as they are in our current histories—the legends about Attila and Charlemagne, or Louis the Pious, where history begins to be altogether fabulous. The most important things of all are overlooked in these writings; for it is really only the histories of the soul that make the present time intelligible.

Anthroposophical spiritual science must throw light into the evolving souls of human beings. *Because we have forgotten how to look into the spiritual, we no longer have any history.* Anyone of sensibility can see that in Martianus Capella the old guides and guardians who used to lead people into the spiritual world have become very thin, very lean ladies. But those whom historians teach us to know as Henry I, Otto I, Otto II, Henry II, and so on—they appear as mere puppets of history, formed after the pattern of those who had grown into the thin and pale ladies, after grammar, rhetoric, dialectic, and the others. When all is said and done the personalities who are enumerated in succession in our histories have no more fat on them than those ladies.

Things must be seen as they really are. Actually the people of today should be yearning to see things as they are. Therefore, it is a duty to describe these things wherever possible, and they can be described today within the Anthroposophical Society. I hope that this society, at least, may some day wake up.

Lecture Two

Dornach, July 28, 1922

In various and complicated ways, we have already seen that the human being can only be understood within the context of the entire universe, out of the whole cosmos. Today we will consider this relationship of the human being to the cosmos from a rather simpler standpoint in order to bring the subject to a certain culmination in later lectures.

The most immediate part of the cosmos surrounding us is, to begin with, what appears to us as the *physical* world. But this physical world actually comes to meet us as the mineral kingdom, at least it confronts us only there in its intrinsic, primal form. Considering the mineral kingdom in the wider sense to include water, air, the phenomena of warmth and the warmth ether, we can study within the mineral kingdom the forces and the essential being of the physical world. This physical world manifests its workings, for instance, in gravity and in magnetic and chemical phenomena. In reality we can only study the physical world within the mineral kingdom. As soon as we come to the plant kingdom, the ideas and concepts we have formed for the physical world are no longer adequate. In modern times no one has felt this truth as intensely as Goethe.[1] As a relatively young man he became acquainted with the plant world from a scientific point of view and sensed immediately that the plant world must be understood with a very different kind of thought and observation than is applicable to the physical world. He encountered the science of plants in the form developed by Linnaeus.[2] This great Swedish naturalist developed botany by observing, above all, the external and minute forms to be found in the individual species and genera. Following these forms he evolved a system in which plants with similar structural characteristics are grouped into genera, so that the various genera and species stand next to each other in the same way as the objects of the mineral kingdom are organized. Goethe was repelled by this aspect of the Linnaean system, by this grouping of individual plant forms. This, said Goethe to himself, is how one observes the minerals and everything of a mineral nature. A different kind of perception must be used for plants. In the case of plants, said Goethe, one would have to proceed in the following way: Here, let us say, is a plant that develops roots, then a stem, then leaves on the stem, and so forth (drawing 1). But it does not always have to be that way. For example, Goethe said to himself, it could be like this (drawing 2):

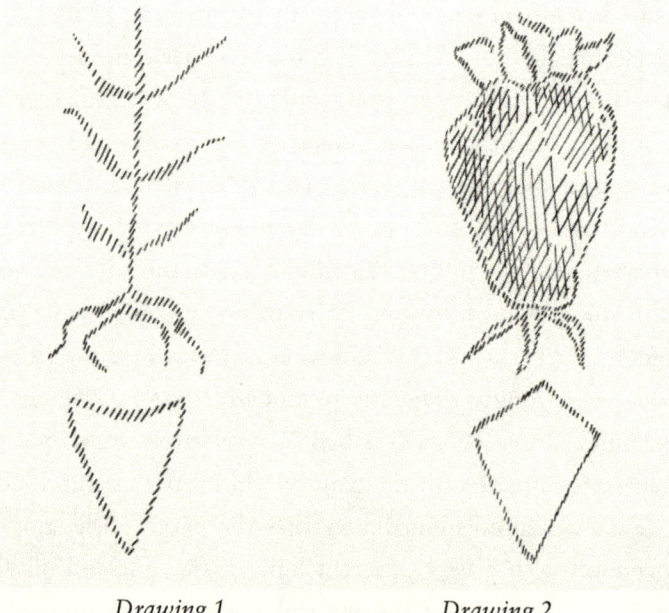

Drawing 1   *Drawing 2*

Lecture Two

Here is the root—but the force that in the first plant (drawing 1) began to develop right in the root is held back here (drawing 2), still enclosed in itself, and therefore does not develop a slender stem that immediately unfolds its leaves but a thick bulbous stem instead. In this way the forces of the leaves go into the thick stem structure and very little remains over to start new leaves or, with time, blossoms. Or again, it may be that a plant develops its roots very sparingly; some of the forces of the roots are left. Such a development would look like this (drawing 3):

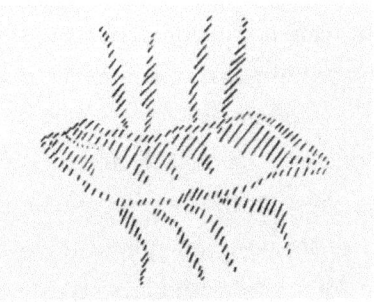

Drawing 3

Then there would be few stalk and leaf starts developing from the plant. All these examples are, however, inwardly the same. In one case the stem is slender and the leaves strongly developed (drawing 1); in another (drawing 2), the stem becomes bulbous and the leaves grow sparingly. The basic idea is the same in all the plants but the idea must be kept inwardly mobile in order to be able to move from one form to the other. Here I must create this form: weak stem, distinct leaves, concentrated leaf force (drawing 1). With the same idea I get a second form: concentrated root force (drawing 2). And again with the same idea I find another, a third form. And so I must create a flexible, mobile concept, through which the whole system of plants becomes a unity.

Whereas Linnaeus set the different forms side by side and observed them as he would observe mineral forms, Goethe, by means of mobile ideas, wanted to grasp the whole system of plant growth as a unity—so that he slipped out of one plant form, as it were, into another form by metamorphosing the idea itself. This kind of observation with mobile ideas was, in Goethe, doubtless the initial impulse toward an imaginative way of observing. Thus we may say that when Goethe approached the system of Linnaeus, he felt that the usual object-oriented way of knowing, although very useful when applied to the physical world of the mineral kingdom, was not adequate for the study of plant life. Confronted with the Linnaean system he felt the necessity for an imaginative means of observation.

In other words, Goethe said to himself: When I look at a plant it is not the physical that I see or, at any rate, that I should see; in a manner of speaking, the physical has become invisible, and I must grasp what I see with ideas very different from those applicable to the mineral kingdom. It is extraordinarily important for us to appreciate this distinction. If we see it in the right way we can say that in the mineral kingdom nature is outwardly visible all around us, while in the plant kingdom physical nature has become invisible. Of course, gravity and all the other forces of physical nature are still at work in the plant kingdom; but they have become invisible while a higher nature has become visible—a higher nature that is inwardly mobile all the time, inwardly alive. What is really visible in the plant is the *etheric* nature. And we are wrong if we say that the physical body of the plant is visible. The physical body of the plant has actually become invisible. What we see is the etheric form.

How then does the visible part of the plant really come into being? If you have a physical body, for instance, a quartz crystal, you can see the physical in an unmediated way. But with a plant you do not really see the physical, you see the etheric form. This etheric form is filled out with physical matter; physical substances live within it. When the plant loses its life and becomes carbon in the Earth you see how the substance of physical carbon remains. It is contained in the plant. We can say, then, that the plant is filled out with the physical but dissolves the physical through the etheric. The etheric is what is actually visible in the plant form. The physical is invisible.

Thus the physical becomes visible for us in the mineral world. In the world of the plants the physical has already become invisible, for what we see is really the etheric made visible through the agency of the physical. We would not, of course, see the plants with our ordinary eyes if the invisible etheric body did not carry within it little granules (an overly simplified and crude expression, to be sure) of physical matter. Through the physical the etheric form becomes visible to us; but this etheric form is what we are really seeing. The physical is, so to speak, only the means whereby we see the etheric. So that the etheric form of a plant is an example of an Imagination, but of an Imagination that is not directly visible in the spiritual world but only becomes visible through physical substances.

What is an Imagination? If you were to ask this, we could answer that the plants are all Imaginations, but as Imaginations they are visible only to imaginative consciousness. That they are also visible to the physical eye is due to the fact that they are filled with physical particles whereby the etheric is rendered visible in a physical way to the physical eye. But if we want to speak correctly we should never say that in the plant we are seeing something physical. In the plants we are seeing genuine Imaginations. We have Imaginations all around us in the forms of the plant world.

But if we now ascend from the world of plants to that of animals, it is no longer sufficient for us to turn to the etheric.

Here we must go a step further. In a sense we can say of the plant that it nullifies the physical and makes manifest the being of the etheric.

Plant: nullifies the physical and manifests the being of the etheric. But when we ascend to the animal, we are not allowed to hold onto the etheric; we must imagine the animal form with the etheric now also nullified. Thus we can say that the animal nullifies the physical (the plant does this, too) and also nullifies the etheric: the animal manifests what can assert itself when the etheric is nullified. When the physical is nullified by the plant the etheric can assert itself. If, then, the etheric, too, is only a filling, granules (again, a crude expression), then the *astral*, which is not within the world of ordinary space but works in ordinary space, can make its being manifest. Therefore, we must say that in the animal the being of the astral is made manifest.

Animal: nullifies the physical, nullifies the etheric, and manifests the being of the astral. Goethe strove with all his power to acquire mobile ideas, mobile concepts, to behold this fluctuating life in the world of the plants. In the plants the etheric is before us because the plant, as it were, drives the etheric out onto the surface. The etheric lives in the form of the plant. But in animals we must recognize the existence of something that is not driven to the surface. The very fact that a plant must remain at the place where it has grown shows that there is nothing in the plant that does not come to the surface and make itself visible. The animal moves about freely. There is something in the animal that does not come to the surface and become visible. This is the astral in the animal, something that cannot be grasped by merely making our ideas mobile, as I explained previously, by merely showing how we move from form to form in the idea itself. This does not suffice for the astral. If we want to understand the astral we must go further and say that something enters into the etheric and is then able, from within outward, to enlarge the form—for example, to make the form nodular or tuberous. In the plant you must always look outside for the cause of the variation in form, for the reasons why the form changes. You must be flexible with your idea. But the merely mobile is not enough to comprehend the animal. To comprehend the animal you have to bring something else into your concepts. If you want to understand how the conceptual activity appropriate for understanding animals must differ from that for plants, then you need more than a mobile concept capable of assuming different forms; the concept itself must receive something inwardly, must take into itself something that it does not contain of itself. This something could be called Inspiration in the forming of concepts. In the organic activity that takes place below our breathing we remain in the activity, so to speak, within ourselves. But when we breathe in, we receive the air from outside; so too if we would comprehend the animal we not only need to have mobile concepts but we must take into these mobile concepts something from the "outside."

Let me explain the difference in another way. If we really want to understand the plant, then we can remain standing still, as it were; we can regard ourselves, even in thought, as stationary beings. And even if we were to remain stationary our whole life long we would still be able to make our concepts mobile enough to grasp the most varied forms in the plant world. But we could never form the idea, the concept of an animal, if we ourselves could not move about. We must be able to move around ourselves if we want to form the concept of an animal. Why?

When you transform the concept of a plant (drawing 1) into a second concept (drawing 2) then you yourself have transformed the concept. But if you then begin running, your concept becomes different through the very act of your running; you yourself must bring life into the concept. That infusion of life is what makes a merely imagined concept into an inspired concept. When it is a plant that is concerned, you can picture yourself inwardly at rest and merely changing the concepts. But if you want to think a true concept of an animal (most people do not like to do this at all because the concept must become inwardly alive; it wriggles within) then you must take the Inspiration, the inner liveliness, into yourself, it is not enough to externally weave sense perceptions from form to form. You cannot think an animal in its totality without taking this inner liveliness into the concept.

This conception of the animal was something that Goethe did not achieve. He did reach the point of being able to say that the plant world is a sum total of concepts, of Imaginations. But with the animals something has to be brought into the concept; with the animal we ourselves have to make the concept inwardly alive. In the case of a plant the Imagination is not itself actually living. This can be seen from the fact that as the plant stands in the ground and grows, its form changes only as the result of external stimuli, and not because of any inner activity. But the animal is, in a manner of speaking, the moving, living concept; with the animal we have to bring in Inspiration, and only through Inspiration can we penetrate to the astral.

When, finally, we ascend to the human being we have to say that he nullifies the physical, the etheric, and the astral and makes the "I"-being manifest.

Humanity: nullifies the physical, nullifies the etheric, nullifies the astral, and manifests the being of the "I." With an animal we must say that what we see is really not the physical but a physically appearing Inspiration. This is the reason why, when the inspiration or breathing of a person is disturbed in some way

Lecture Two

it very easily assumes an animal form. Try sometime to remember some of the figures that appear in nightmares. Very many of them appear in animal forms. Animal forms are filled with Inspirations.

We can grasp the human "I" only through *Intuition*. Truly, in reality, the human "I" can be grasped through only Intuition. In the animal we see Inspiration; in the human being we actually see the "I," the Intuition. We speak falsely when we say that we see the physical body of an animal. We do not see the physical body at all. It has been dissolved away, nullified, it merely makes the Inspiration visible to us; and the etheric body has likewise been dissolved away, nullified. With an animal we are actually seeing the astral body externally by means of the physical and the etheric. And with the human being we perceive the "I." What we actually see there before us is not the physical body, for it is invisible—and so too are the etheric body and the astral body. What we see in a human being is the "I" formed externally in a physical way. This is why people appear to outer visual perception in their flesh color—a color found nowhere else, just as one's "I" is not found in any other being. Therefore, if we want to express ourselves correctly, we would say that we can completely comprehend the human being only when we think of that person as consisting of physical body, etheric body, astral body, and the "I." What we see before us is the "I," whereas the astral, etheric, and physical bodies exist invisibly within.

Now, we really comprehend the human being only by considering the matter a little more closely. What we see to begin with is merely the "outside" of the "I." But the "I" is perceptible in its true form only inwardly, only through Intuition. But something of this "I" is also noticed by humans in their ordinary, conscious life—that is, in abstract thoughts that animals do not have, because they do not have an "I." Animals do not have the ability to think abstract thoughts, because they do not have an "I." Therefore, we can say that in the human form and figure we see the earthly incarnation of the "I" externally; when we experience ourselves from inwardly, in our abstract thoughts, there we have the "I." But these are merely thoughts; they are pictures, not realities.

Now consider the astral body, which is present though nullified. We come to the member that cannot be seen externally but that we can see if we look at a person in movement and from those movements begin to understand that person's form. Here we need to practice this kind of observation: Think of a small, dwarflike, and thickset man who walks about on short legs. You will understand his movement by observing his stout legs, which he thrusts forward like little pillars. A tall, lanky man with very long legs will move very differently. Observing in this way, you will see unity between movement and form. You can train yourself to observe this unity in other aspects of human movement and form. For example, a man with a forehead sloping backward and a very prominent chin moves his head differently from someone with a receding chin and a strikingly projecting forehead. You will see connections everywhere between the forms and movements of human beings if you simply observe them as they stand before you, gathering impressions of their flesh and its color, and how they hold themselves when in repose. You are observing a person's "I" when you watch what passes from the form into movements and back again into form.

Study the human hand sometime. How differently people with long or short fingers handle their tools. Movement passes over into form, form into movement. Here you are visualizing, as it were, a shadow of the astral body expressed through external, physical means. But, you see, as I am describing it to you now, it is a primitive Inspiration. Most people do not think of observing people who walk about, as, for example, Fichte walked the streets of Jena.[3] Anyone who saw Fichte walking through the streets of Jena could also have sensed the movement and the formative process that were in his speech organs and came to expression particularly when he wanted his words to carry conviction although they were in his speech organs all the time. Inspiration, at least in an elementary form, is required in order to see this.

But when we see from within what we have thus seen from without, which I have told you is perceptible by means of a primitive kind of Inspiration, what we find is, in essence, the human life of fantasy permeated with feeling. It is the realm where abstract thoughts are inwardly experienced. Memory pictures, too, when they arise, live in this element.

Seen externally, the "I" is expressed, for example, in the flesh color, but also in other forms, for example, in the countenance. Otherwise we would never be able to speak of a physiognomy. If, for example, the corners of one's mouth droop when one's face is in repose, this is definitely connected karmically with the configuration of one's "I" in this incarnation. Seen from the inside, however, abstract thoughts are present here. The astral body reveals itself externally in the character of the movements, inwardly in fantasy or in the pictures of fantasy that appear to the human being. The astral body itself more or less avoids observation, the etheric body still more so.

The etheric body is really not visible from outside, or at most only becomes visible in physical manifestation in very exceptional cases. It can, however, become externally visible when a person sweats—when a person sweats the etheric body becomes visible outwardly. But you see, Imagination is required in order to relate the process of sweating to the whole human being. Paracelsus[4] was one who made this connection. For him, not only the manner but the substance of the sweat differed in individual human beings. For Paracelsus, the whole human being—the etheric nature of the entire human being—was expressed in this way. Generally speaking, then, there is very little external expression of the etheric. Inwardly, on the other hand, it is experienced all the more, namely in feeling. The whole life of feeling, inwardly experienced, is what is living in the etheric body when this body is active from within, so that one experiences it from within. The life of feeling is always accompanied by inner secretion. To observation of the etheric body in the human being it appears that the liver, for instance, sweats, that the stomach sweats—that every organ sweats and secretes. The etheric life of the human being lives in this process of inner secretion. Around the liver, around the heart, there is a cloud of sweat, all is enveloped in mist and cloud. This needs to be understood imaginatively. When Paracelsus spoke about the sweat of the human being he did not say that it is only on the surface. He said rather that sweat permeates the whole human being, that it is one's etheric body that is seen when the physical is allowed to fall away from sight. This inner experience of the etheric body is, as I have said, the life of feeling.

And the external experience of the physical body—this, too, is by no means immediately perceptible. True, we become aware of the physical part of human corporeality when, for example, we take a child into our arms. It is heavy, just as a stone is heavy. That is a physical experience; we perceive something that belongs to the physical world. If someone gives us a box on the ears there is, apart from the moral experience, a physical experience, too—a blow, an impact. But as something physical it is actually only an elastic blow, as when one billiard ball impacts another. The physical element must always be kept separate from the other, the moral element. But if we go on to perceive this physical element inwardly, in the same way we inwardly perceive the external manifestation of the life of feeling, then in the merely physical processes we experience inwardly the human will. The

Lecture Two

human will is what brings the human being together with the cosmos in a simple, straightforward way.

You see, when we look around us for Inspiration we find it in the forms of the animals. The manifold variety of animal forms is the basis for our perceptions in Inspiration. You will realize from this fact that when Inspirations are seen in their pure, original form, without being filled with physical corporeality, that these Inspirations can then represent something essentially higher than animals. And they can, too. But Inspirations that are present in the spiritual world in their pure state may also appear to us in animal-like forms.

In the times of the old atavistic clairvoyance people sought to portray in animal forms the Inspirations that came to them. The form of the sphinx, for example, was intended to create a picture of something that had been seen in Inspiration. We are dealing, therefore, with superhuman beings when we speak of animal forms in the purely spiritual world. During the days of atavistic clairvoyance—and this continued in the first four Christian centuries, in any case, still at the time of The Mystery of Golgotha—it was no mere symbolism in the ordinary sense, but a genuine inner knowledge that caused artists to portray, in the forms of animals, spiritual beings who were accessible to Inspiration.

It was in complete accordance with this practice when the Holy Spirit was portrayed in the form of a dove by those who had received Inspiration. How must we think of it today when the Holy Spirit is said to have appeared in the form of a dove? We must say to ourselves: Those people who spoke in this way were inspired, in the old atavistic sense. They saw him in this form as an Inspiration in that realm of pure spirit where the Holy Spirit revealed himself to them.

And how would the contemporaries of The Mystery of Golgotha who were endowed with atavistic clairvoyance have characterized the Christ? Perhaps they had seen him outwardly as a man. To see him as a human being in the spiritual world they would have needed Intuition. And people who were able to see his "I" in the world of Intuition were not present at the time of The Mystery of Golgotha. That was not possible for them. But they could still see him in atavistic Inspiration. They would, then, have used animal imagery, even to express Christ. "Behold the Lamb of God!" This was true and correct language for that time. It is language we must come to understand if we are to grasp what Inspiration is or to see, by means of Inspiration, what can become manifest in the spiritual world. "Behold the lamb of God!" It is important for us to recognize once again what is imaginative, what is inspired, and what is intuitive, and thereby to find our way into the language that echoes down to us from ancient times.

In terms of the ancient powers of vision this way of language presents us with realities. But we must learn to express such realities in the way they were still expressed, for example, at the time of The Mystery of Golgotha, and to feel that they are justified and natural. Only in this way will we be able to grasp the meaning of what was represented, for example, over in Asia as the winged cherubim, in Egypt as the sphinx, and what is presented to us as a dove and even as Christ, the Lamb. In ancient times Christ was again and again portrayed through Inspiration, or better said, through inspired Imagination.

Lecture Three

Dornach, July 29, 1922

Yesterday I tried to show you how a simple way can be found to envisage the human being's relationships to the cosmos in terms of body, soul, and spirit. I concluded yesterday's lecture by building up to certain imaginative pictures, through which I wanted to draw attention to certain things, showing how inspired Imaginations are truly and correctly expressed in imaginative pictures such as "Christ as the Lamb of God." I wanted to show that when such pictures were formed—indeed, when they were voiced with complete understanding and used for the life of the human soul—a real consciousness was present of how human beings work upward from ordinary consciousness to conscious experiences in the soul, experiences that connect them to the spiritual world. I pointed to the fact that, during the first four Christian centuries, what we could call the Christian teaching still carried the impression that it was based everywhere on a real perception of the spiritual, that even the secrets of Christianity were presented as they could actually be seen by those who had developed their soul life to spiritual vision.

After the fourth century AD, understanding of direct expressions of the spiritual faded increasingly from ordinary consciousness. With contact between the Germanic peoples from the north and the Latin and Greek peoples of the south during those early days of growth for Western culture, we see how these difficulties of understanding continuously increased. We must be fully aware that during the time immediately following the fourth century, people still looked with reverent devotion at those imaginations when Christian views were presented in earlier times. Tradition was revered and so, too, were the pictures that had come down to posterity through tradition. But the progressing human spirit continued to assume new forms.

Therefore, human beings were led to say that, yes, tradition has handed down to us pictures, such as the dove for the Holy Spirit and the Lamb of God for Christ himself, but how are we come to understand them? Out of this impossibility—or rather, from the faith born with a conviction of the impossibility of the human spirit ever achieving perception of the spiritual worlds through its own powers—the Scholastic doctrine arose, saying that the human spirit, which can achieve knowledge of the sensory world by its own power, can also reach conclusions derived directly from concepts of the sensory world, but that human beings must simply accept without comprehension revelations of what can be revealed to us concerning the suprasensory world.

However, this twofold form of faith in the human soul life did not develop without difficulties. There was knowledge limited to the earthly on the one hand, while on the other there was knowledge of the suprasensory, attainable only through faith or belief. Nevertheless, it was always felt, though somewhat dimly, that the human relationship to suprasensory knowledge could not be the same as it was in ancient times. Concerning this feeling, just after the fourth century people said to themselves that, in a certain sense, the suprasensory world could still be reached by the human soul, but that it is not given to all to develop their souls to such heights; most people have to be content with simply accepting many of the old revelations.

As I said, people revered these old revelations so much that they did not wish to measure them against a standard of human knowledge that no longer reached up to them. At least, people did not believe that human knowledge was capable of rising to the level of revelation. The strict Scholastic doctrine concerning the division of human knowledge was, in fact accepted only gradually. Actually, it was not until the tenth, eleventh, twelfth, and thirteenth centuries of the Middle Ages that this Scholastic tenet was fully acknowledged. Until then, there was still a certain wavering in peoples' minds over the possibility of rising to such knowledge, which people could still achieve at this late date, up to the level of what belongs to the suprasensory world.

The triumph of the Scholastic view meant that, in contrast to earlier times, a powerful revolution had taken place. You see, in earlier times—say, during the very first Christian centuries—if individuals had struggled through to Christianity and then approached the mystery of divine providence or the mystery of the transubstantiation of bread and wine into the body and blood of Christ, they would have said that this is difficult to understand, but there are those who can develop their souls so that they understand such matters. They would have said that, if I assume the omniscience of the Godhead, then this omniscient being must actually also know whether one human being is damned for all time or another will enter blessedness.

However, such a person might have said that this hardly seems to agree with the fact that people need not inevitably sin and that, if they do sin, they will then be damned—that if they do not sin, they will not be damned or that no one will be damned who does penance for a sin. We must say, therefore, that individuals, through the way they conduct their lives, can either make themselves into the damned through sin or into the blessed by being without sin. Moreover, an omniscient God must already know whether individuals are destined for damnation or blessedness.

Such would have been the considerations of someone so confronted in the earliest Christian centuries. However, in these early Christian centuries that person would not have said that one must therefore argue over whether God foresees the damnation or the blessedness of human beings. One would have said instead that, if I were initiated I would be able to understand that although an individual may or may not sin, God knows nevertheless who will be damned and who will be blessed. This is the way someone living in the first Christian centuries would have thought.

Similarly, if someone had told people that, through transubstantiation and celebration of the Eucharist, bread and wine are transformed into the body and blood of Christ, they would have said they didn't understand this, but if they were initiated they would. In ancient times, a person would have thought that what we can observe in the sensory world are mere appearances and not reality, and that the reality lies behind in the spiritual world. As long as we are in the sensory world, the world of illusions, it is a contradiction to say that someone can either sin or not sin and that the omniscient God nevertheless knows in advance whether an individual will be damned or blessed, but as soon as we enter the spiritual world it is no longer a contradiction. There we experience how it is possible that God, nevertheless, sees ahead. Likewise, people would have said that, in the physical world of senses, it is contradictory to say that bread and wine, whose outward appearance remains the same, become the body and blood of Christ after the transubstantiation, but when we are initiated we will understand this, because then, in our soul lives we are within the spiritual world. This is how people thought in ancient times.

Then came the struggles in human souls. On the one hand human souls found themselves increasingly separated and torn

Lecture Three

away from the spiritual world. The whole trend of culture was to grant authority only to reason, which of course does not reach into the spiritual world. All kinds of uncertainties concerning the suprasensory worlds developed form those struggles.

When we study the symptoms of history, we can find the points where such uncertainties enter the world quite starkly. I have often spoken of the Scottish monk Scotus Eriugena, who lived in France at the court of Charles the Bald during the ninth century.[1] At court he was regarded as a veritable miracle of wisdom. Charles the Bald, and all those who thought as he did, turned to Scotus Eriugena in all matters of religion and also of science whenever they wanted a verdict. Now the way Scotus Eriugena stood opposed to the other monks of his time shows how fiercely the battle was then raging between reason, which felt itself limited to the world of sense, along with a few conclusions derived from that world, and the traditions that had been handed down from the spiritual world in the form of dogmas.

Thus in the ninth century we see two personalities confronting one another: Scotus Eriugena and the monk Gottschalk,[2] who uncompromisingly asserted the doctrine that God has perfect foreknowledge of an individual's future damnation or blessedness. This teaching was gradually embodied in the formula: God has destined one portion of humanity for blessedness and another for damnation. The doctrine was formulated as Augustine himself had formulated it. Following his teaching of predestination, one part of humanity is destined for blessedness, another part for damnation.[3] And the monk Gottschalk taught that it is indeed so; God has destined one portion of the human race for blessedness and another for damnation, but no portion is predestined for sin. Thus, for external understanding, Gottschalk was teaching a contradiction.

During the ninth century, the strife was extraordinarily fierce. At a synod in Mainz, for instance, Gottschalk's writing was declared heretical, and he was scourged because of this teaching. However, although Gottschalk had been scourged and imprisoned on account of this doctrine he was able to claim that he had no other desire than to reaffirm the teaching of Augustine in its genuine form. Many French bishops and monks, in particular, realized that Gottschalk was not teaching anything other than what Augustine had already taught. And so a monk such as Gottschalk stood before the people of his time teaching from the traditions of the old mystery knowledge. However, those who now wished to understand everything with the dawning intellect were simply unable to understand and therefore contested his teaching. But there were others who adhered more to reverence for the old and were decidedly on the side of a theologian like Gottschalk.

It is extremely difficult for people today to understand that things like this could be the subject of bitter strife. When such teachings did not please parties with authority their author was publicly scourged and imprisoned even though he might be, and in this case was, eventually vindicated. For it was precisely the orthodox believers who ranged themselves on the side of Gottschalk, and his teaching remained the orthodox Catholic doctrine. Charles the Bald, because of his relationship to Scotus Eriugena, naturally turned to him for a verdict. Scotus Eriugena did not decide for Gottschalk's teaching but as follows: The Godhead is to be found in the evolution of humanity; actually, evil can only *appear* to have existence, otherwise evil, too, would have to be found in God. Since God can be only Good, evil must be a nothing; but human beings cannot be united with "nothing." This is why Scotus Eriugena spoke out against the teaching of Gottschalk.

Lecture Three

But the teaching of Scotus Eriugena, which was more or less the same as that of pantheists today, was in turn condemned by the orthodox Church and his writings were only later rediscovered. Everything reminiscent of his teaching was burned and he came to be regarded as the real heretic. When he made known the views he had explained to Charles the Bald, the adherents of Gottschalk—who were now again respected—declared: Scotus Eriugena is actually only a babbler who adorns himself with every kind of ornament of external science and who actually knows nothing at all about the inner mysteries of the suprasensory.

Another theologian wrote about the body and blood of Christ in *De Corpore et Sanguine Domini*.[4] In this writing he said something that, for the initiates of old, had been an understandable teaching: that in actual fact bread and wine can be changed into the real body and the real blood of Christ. This writing, too, was laid before Charles the Bald. Scotus Eriugena did not write an actual refutation but in his works we have many a hint of the decision he reached, namely, that this, the orthodox Catholic teaching of the transubstantiation of bread and wine into the body and blood of Christ, must be modified because it is not understandable to the human mind. This was how Scotus Eriugena was able to express himself, even in his day.

In short, the conflict concerning the human soul's relationship to the suprasensory world raged fiercely in the ninth century, and it was exceedingly difficult for serious minds of that time to find their bearings. For Christian dogmas contained everywhere deposits, as it were, of ancient truths of initiation, but people were powerless to understand them. What had been uttered in external words was put to the test. These words could only have been intelligible to a soul that had developed itself up into the spiritual world. The external words were tested against what had come to the consciousness of people at that time as a result of the development of human reason. And the most intense battles ensued within the Christian life of Europe from the testing of that time.

Where were these inner experiences leading? They were tending in the direction of a duality entirely absent in former times. In earlier times, human beings looked into the sensory world and as they looked their faculties enabled them simultaneously to behold the spiritual pervading the phenomena of this sensory world. People saw the spiritual along with the phenomena of the world of senses. The people of ancient times certainly did not see bread and wine in the same way that people in the ninth century AD saw them—that is, as being merely matter. In ancient times the material and spiritual were seen together. So, too, the people in ancient times didn't have concepts and ideas as intellectual as those already possessed by people living in the ninth century.

The thinness and abstraction of the concepts and ideas in the ninth century were not present earlier. What people experienced earlier as ideas and concepts was still such that concepts and ideas were like real objects with essential being. Concepts and ideas in ancient times were not thin and abstract, but full of living reality, of objective being. I have told you how subjects such as grammar, rhetoric, dialectic, arithmetic, geometry, music, and astrology gradually became entirely abstract. In ancient times, the human relationship to these sciences was such that, as people lived into them, they entered a relationship with real, actual beings. But by the ninth century, and even more later on, the sciences of grammar, rhetoric, dialectic, and so on had become wholly thin and abstract, without living content of being—almost, one might say, like mere pieces of clothing in comparison with what had formerly been present.

This process of abstraction continued. Abstraction increasingly became a quality of concepts and ideas while concrete

Lecture Three

reality increasingly became nothing more than the external sensory world. These two streams, which we see in the ninth century influenced people to fight such devastating soul battles—these two streams have persisted into modern times. In some instances we still experience their conflict sharply, in other instances the conflict receives less emphasis.

These tendencies in the evolution of humanity stand with a living clarity in the contrast between Goethe and Schiller.[5] Yesterday, I spoke about the fact that Goethe, having studied the botany of Linnaeus, was compelled to evolve really living concepts and pictures of the plants—concepts capable of change and metamorphosis, which, for this reason, came near to being Imaginations. But I also drew your attention to the fact that Goethe stumbled when his mind tried to rise from plant life to the animal world of sentient experience. He could reach Imagination but not Inspiration. He saw the external phenomena. With the minerals he had no cause to advance to Imagination; with plant life he did, but got no further because abstract concepts and ideas were not his strong point. Goethe did not philosophize in the manner customary in his day. Therefore, he was unable to express in abstract concepts what is found at a spiritual level higher than that of the plants.

But Schiller philosophized. He even learned how to philosophize from Kant, although the Kantian way ultimately became too confused for him and he left it.[6] Schiller philosophized without the degree of abstraction that prevents concepts from reaching actual being. And when we study Goethe and Schiller together this is precisely what we feel to be the fundamental opposition never really bridged between them, the opposition that was only smoothed over through the greatness of soul, the essential humanity that lived in both of them. However, this fundamental difference of approach showed itself in the last decade of the eighteenth century when Goethe and Schiller were both occupied with this question: How the human beings achieve an existence worthy of their dignity?

Schiller asked the question in his own way, as abstract thought, and what he had to say about it appeared in his book *On the Aesthetic Education of Man*. He says there that human beings are, on the one hand, subject to the necessity implicit in logic and reason. We have no freedom when we follow the necessity of reason. Human freedom goes under in the necessity of reason, but neither are we free when we surrender ourselves wholly to the senses—to the necessity implicit in the senses. In this area, instincts and natural urges coerce us, and again we are not free. In both directions—toward the spirit and toward nature—human beings become slaves, unfree.

Schiller concludes that as human beings we can become free only when we view nature as if it were a living being, as if nature had spirit and soul within it—in other words, if we lift nature to a higher level. But then we must also bring the necessity implicit in reason right down into nature. We must, as it were, regard nature as if it had reason; but then the rigidity of necessity and logic vanish from reason. When human beings expresses themselves in pictures they give form, creating instead of logically analyzing and synthesizing. As we create in this way, we remove from nature the element of necessity caused by the mere senses. But this achievement of freedom, said Schiller, can be expressed only in artistic creation and aesthetic appreciation. Those who simply confront nature passively are under the sway of the necessity implicit in nature—instincts, natural desires, and urges. If we set our mind to work, we must follow the necessity implicit in logic if we do not wish to be untrue to the human. When we combine the two, nature and logic, then the necessity implicit in reason subsides, then reason yields something of its necessity to the sensory world,

Lecture Three

and the sensory world of nature yields something of its instinctual compulsion. The human being is represented in works of sculpture, for instance, as if spirit itself were already contained in the sensory world. We lead the spirit down into the sensuality of material nature while leading the sensuality of material nature up to the spirit, and the creation through images, the beautiful, arises. Only while creating or appreciating the beautiful does the human being live in freedom.

In writing *On the Aesthetic Education of Man*, Schiller strove with all the power of his soul to discover when it is possible for human beings to be free. He found the only possibility of realizing human freedom in the life of beautiful appearances. We must flee crude reality if we desire to be free—that is, if we wish to achieve an existence worthy of being human. This is what Schiller really meant, though he may not have stated it explicitly. Real freedom can be attained only in appearance, or semblance.

Nietzsche, who was steeped in all these matters, nevertheless could not penetrate through to an actual perception of the spirit. In his first book, *The Birth of Tragedy from the Spirit of Music*,[7] he wanted to show that the Greeks created art in order to have something through that, as free human beings in dignity, they might be able to rise above the reality presented by the external senses, the reality in which human beings can never achieve their true dignity. They raised themselves above the reality of things to achieve the possibility of freedom in appearances, in artistic appearances. Thus Nietzsche interpreted Greek culture. Here, Nietzsche merely expressed, in a radical form, what was already contained in Schiller's letters on the aesthetic education of humanity.

Therefore, we can say that Schiller lived in an abstract spirituality, but that at the same time there lived within him the impulse to grant human beings their true dignity. Just look at the sublimity, the greatness, of his letters on aesthetic education. They are worthy of the very highest admiration. In terms of poetic feeling, in terms of the power of soul, they are really greater than all his other works. When we think of the sum total of his achievements, these letters are the greatest of them all. But Schiller had to struggle with them from an abstract point of view, for he, too, had arrived at the intellectualism characterizing the spiritual life of the West. And from this standpoint he could not reach true reality. He could only reach the shining appearance of the beautiful.

When Goethe read Schiller's letters on the aesthetic education of humanity, it was not easy for him to find his way around in them. Goethe was actually not very adept at following the processes of abstract reasoning but he, too, was concerned with the problem of how humans can achieve true dignity, how spiritual beings must work together to give human beings dignity so that, awakened to the spiritual world, they can live into it.

Schiller could not emerge from the picture, or image, to the reality. What Schiller had said in his letters, Goethe also wanted to say, but in his own way. He did so in the pictures and imagery in his "Fairy Tale of the Green Snake and the Beautiful Lily."[8] In all the figures in this fairy tale we are to see powers of the soul working together to impart to humans their true dignity, in freedom. But Goethe was unable to find the way from what he had been able to express in Imaginations up to the truly spiritual. Hence, he got no further than the fairy tale, a picture, a kind of higher symbolism. It was, it is true, full of an extraordinary amount of life; still, it was only a kind of symbolism. Schiller formed abstract concepts, but remaining with appearance he could not get into reality. Goethe, trying to understand human beings in their freedom, created many pictures, vividly concrete pictures, but they could not get him into reality either. He remained stuck with mere descriptions of the world of sense. You see, his description of the sense images in "The Fairy Tale of the Green Snake and the Beautiful Lily" are wonderfully beautiful, yet it cannot be said that the final freeing of the crippled prince is intuitively obvious and real; it is only symbolically real. Neither of the two contrasting streams expressed in the personalities of Goethe and Schiller, could find a way into the real experience of the spiritual world. Both were striving from opposite sides to penetrate into the spiritual world, but could not get in.

What was really going on? What I am going to say may seem strange. Nevertheless, those who approach these matters without psychological bias will have to agree with the following.

Think of the two streams present in Scholasticism. For one, there is the knowledge from reason, creating its content out of the world of sense but not penetrating through to reality. This stream flows on through manifold forms, passing from one personality to another, also down to Schiller. Scholasticism held that one can only obtain ideas from the world of sense—and Schiller was drawn into this way of knowing. But Schiller was far too complete a human being to regard the sensuality of physical matter as compatible with true human dignity. Scholastic knowledge merely extracts ideas out of the world of sense. Schiller's solution was to let go of the world of sense so that only ideas remain. But with ideas alone he could not reach reality—he only reached beautiful appearances. He struggled with this problem: What should be done with this Scholastic knowledge that human beings have produced from themselves, so that they can somehow be given their dignity? His answer was that we can no longer stay with reality, that we must take refuge in the beauty of appearances. Thus you see how the stream of Scholastic knowledge from reason found its way to Schiller.

Goethe did not care much for this kind of knowledge. Actually he was much more excited by knowledge as revelation. You may find this strange; nevertheless, it is true. And even if he did not adhere to those Catholic dogmas, the necessity of which became clear to him as he was trying to complete *Faust*, and express them artistically, even if he did not adhere to the Catholic dogmas of his youth, still he held to things pertaining to the suprasensory world at the level he was able to reach. To speak to Goethe of a faith—this, in a way, made him furious. When, in Goethe's youth, Jacobi spoke to him about belief, about faith, he replied: I keep to vision, to seeing.[9] Goethe didn't want to hear anything about belief or faith. Those who claim him for any particular faith simply do not understand him at all. He was out to see.

Furthermore, he was actually on the way from his Imaginations to Inspirations and Intuitions. In this way he could naturally never have become a theologian of the Middle Ages, but he could have become like an ancient seer of the divine, a seer of suprasensory worlds. He was certainly on the way, but was simply unable to ascend high enough. He only got far enough to see the suprasensory in the world of the plants. When he studied the plant world he was actually able to see the spiritual and the sensible next to one another as had the initiates in the ancient mysteries. But Goethe got no further than the plant world.

What, then, was the only thing he could do? He could only apply to the whole world of the suprasensory the pictorial method, the symbolism, the imaginative contemplation that he had learned to apply to the plants. And so, when he spoke of the soul life in his fairy tale he was only able to achieve an imaginative presentation of the world.

Whenever "The Fairy Tale of the Green Snake and the Beautiful Lily" mentions anything concerning plant life, anything that can be approached with Imaginations such as those developed by Goethe for the world of plants, then the writing is particularly beautiful. Just allow everything expressed in the style of Imaginations of the plant world in this fairy tale to work on you and you will feel a wonderful beauty. Actually, the rest of the fairy tale's contents also have a tendency to become plant-like. The central female figure, upon whom so much depends, he names Lily. Goethe does not manage to imbue her with real, potent life; he manages only to give her a kind of plant existence. And if you look at all the figures appearing in the fairy tale, actually they all lead a kind of plant existence. Where it becomes necessary to raise them to a higher level, they become mere symbols, and their existence is mere appearance at that level. The kings that appear in the fairy tale aren't properly real either. They, too, manage to achieve only a plant-like existence; they only claim to have another kind of life, as well. Something would have to be *in-spired* into the ancient king, the silver king, and the bronze king before they could really live in the spiritual world.

Thus Goethe lived out a life of knowledge as revelation, as suprasensory knowledge, which he has only mastered up to a certain level. Schiller lived out the other kind of knowledge—that of reason—which was developed by Scholasticism. But he could not bear this knowledge because he wanted to follow it into reality and it could lead him only as far as the reality of the beauty in appearances.

One can say that the inner truth of the two personalities made them so upright that neither one said more than he was truly able to say. Thus, Goethe depicts the life of the soul as if it were a kind of vegetation, and Schiller portrays the free individual as if a free human being could live only aesthetically. An aesthetic society, as the social challenge, is what Schiller brings forward at the end of the letters on the aesthetic education of humanity. If human beings are to become free, says Schiller, let them live so that society manifests itself as beauty. In Goethe's relationship to Schiller we see how these streams live on. What they would have needed was the ascent from Imagination to Inspiration in Goethe, and the enlivening of abstract concepts with the imaginative world in Schiller. Only then could they have completely come together.

When we look into the souls of both of them, we would have to say that both possessed qualities that could lead them into a world of spirit. Goethe struggled constantly with what he called "religious inclinations," or "piety." When asked, "To which of the existing religions do you confess?" Schiller replied "To none." And when he was asked why, he replied, "For religious reasons!"[10]

As the suprasensory world flows into the human soul from knowledge that is actually experienced, we see how, especially for enlightened spirits, religion itself also flows into the soul. Thus religion will once again have to be attained—through the transformation of the merely intellectual knowledge of today into spiritual knowledge .

Lecture Four

Dornach, July 30, 1922

Once again, we want to look back at those principles of initiation described in yesterday's lecture as having been paralyzed by the advancing intellectualization of culture. Looking back we shall see how those people, in whom these older, atavistic principles of initiation were still alive, confronted Christianity. Out of their perceptions they formulated what subsequently became the contents of dogma and, as such, could no longer be understood after about the eighth or ninth century.

We need only remember that, before The Mystery of Golgotha, the impulse of the true principle of the human self, the "I," was essentially missing in human civilization. Human beings were, of course, always organized in such a way as to have the "I" principle within them; furthermore, they were created to shape outer and inner being from the "I" principle. However, people came to feel and become conscious of the essence and power of the "I" only slowly and by degrees. Thus, we can say that—although human beings, even before The Mystery of Golgotha, consisted of physical, etheric, astral bodies and the "I"—human consciousness did not include within it this "I"-being; the "I" had been more or less unconscious.

In those ancient times, people walked the Earth but, basically, did not live with full "I"-consciousness. However, it is really not possible for the "I" to be active in the human being unless the physical body is no longer developing in its full, original freshness. Those human beings who were still unconscious of their "I" developed their physical bodies in greater freshness than those who had entered into a full consciousness of the "I." This arrival of the full consciousness of the "I" did not occur suddenly; it was taking place both before and after The Mystery of Golgotha, but it is clearly perceptible to a spiritual-scientific observation of history.

What can be maintained in its full freshness in the human physical, etheric, and astral bodies—that can be maintained only so long as something from the divine, spiritual nature is flowing into the human being from the cosmos. But we could never have become free beings if the "I" had not appeared on the scene, if the divine-spiritual had not ceased to flow into us in the old sense. Human beings became free only through achieving, at the same time, mastery of the "I" within their consciousness. But that was possible only after humanity became involved in the realm of abstract thoughts, which are, however, really corpses of the spiritual world. I have already pointed this out in these lectures.

Just as a corpse is left over from our physical nature when we die on Earth, likewise a corpse remains from the being of soul and spirit that we were in the spiritual world before coming down into the physical world. However, this has been true only since human beings have been equipped with "I"-consciousness; thoughts, abstract thoughts, represent this corpse. When we learn to take hold of abstract thoughts, we take hold of the corpse of our spiritual and soul being as it was before our descent into the earthly world. But a precondition for taking hold of that corpse of our spiritual and soul being is that something of the dying and paralyzing principle of death must enter our physical body.

Indeed, the evolution of humankind is such that our nature has changed in the course of human development on Earth. The bodies of human beings in ancient times were different from those of the newer bodies. The bodies of old were such that within them human beings were unfree, but as they moved about, all the freshness of primal being was manifested in their physical, etheric, and astral activities. Thus we can say that, in the civilized world, we already live in a period of the evolution of humanity when the body is beginning inwardly to decay. We attain our freedom precisely through this decaying body, which is the base for our intellectual, abstract thoughts. Through this decaying body, human beings have attained all that people are so proud of today as intellectually imbued scientists.

Considering this, we must say that before The Mystery of Golgotha full consciousness of the self as an "I" was not yet present in human beings on the Earth. Nevertheless, in those times there were a few people who had already developed full "I"-consciousness through the mystery cults; they were called initiates. We have already said much concerning what happened to those who underwent initiation in the places of the ancient mysteries, how they ascended to the experience of the fully conscious "I" at a time when it was the general condition of humankind not yet to have a fully conscious "I." But initiates of old could ascend to the fully conscious "I," because something entered them through the sacred enactments in the mysteries, something that had been felt and experienced in all ancient civilizations as the eternal Father in the cosmos. When initiates, or mystics, had reached a certain point of initiation in the ancient mysteries, they had an experience that allowed them to say to themselves (imagining such an initiate of the ancient Hebrew civilization): "The Father lives in me."

Initiates would characterize what had happened within them through initiation as follows: The nature of human beings in general is such that the Father indeed sustains and bears them, but the Father does not enter their consciousness and does not kindle their consciousness to an experience of the "I." To ordinary human beings, the Father gives only the spirit of breath; he breathes the breath that is the living soul in the human being. But those initiates felt that the living soul breathed into a person was a special spiritual reality, the living Father principle of the cosmos that also entered the human being. Then, once this divine Father principle had entered such initiates of the ancient Hebrew world and they had become conscious of it, they could say with full justification what the "I" meant to them: "I am the I AM."

Such individuals who walked among ancient peoples—because the divine Father principle lived within them—were qualified to speak the "I," which was the name of the Godhead, the Father God, that could not be spoken in the entire ancient world. Such persons were viewed as representatives of the Father on the Earth. Those initiates were called the Fathers who walked among the peoples. They were called Fathers, because they represented the divine principle of the Father to other human beings. It was said of them that the divine Father had entered into them in the mysteries. Thus the mysteries were seen as the places within the earthly world where the principle could develop that otherwise only weaves and surges externally through the entire cosmos. Within the mystery centers and through the mystery centers, a tabernacle was built in the human being for the divine Father principle. Human beings themselves became tabernacles for the divine Father principle.

Through the mysteries human beings felt the surge of God the Father through the earthly world; and looking out into the cosmos, into the great world beyond, they called it the macrocosm, the great world, inasmuch as they thought of it as permeated by and woven through and through by the divine Father principle. They looked then to the mystery centers, within which a tabernacle had been built for this Father God, within which human beings had themselves become tabernacles of the Father God through initiation; and they called the mysteries, and what a human being had become through the mysteries, the little world, the microcosm. This distinction persisted even into the days of Goethe, for when Goethe became a member of certain lodges he picked up the phrase, "The great world and the little world." By "great world" he understood the macrocosm and by "little world," the lodge that was, for him, an image of the "great world."[1]

All of this entered into another phase when The Mystery of Golgotha was drawing near in the evolution of humanity. Hence, something essentially different had to be considered. During The Mystery of Golgotha, there were human beings walking on the Earth who experienced within themselves something of the independent "I." The consciousness of the "I" had begun to enter into human beings. But at the same time something else began to appear: The human physical body began to be inwardly brittle, to decay. And so at this time, in the middle of Earth evolution, human evolution faced a great danger. There was the danger of more and more losing connection with the spiritual world and now there was the danger that the physical body could increasingly decay and fall apart.

To help with this danger the being we know as the Christ resolved to pour himself into Jesus of Nazareth just as the divine Father principle had poured into the initiates in earlier times. This divine Father principle had poured into the initiates. In this way the "I" was enkindled in, and added to, the physical body, etheric body, and astral body. As I have already said, only those into whom the divine Father had entered were allowed to speak the "I," which was itself the unutterable name of God.

But now, in the middle of Earth evolution there lived human beings who were beginning to say "I" of themselves, human beings who had raised the "I" into consciousness. The Son principle, the Christ principle, now entered into just such a human being, into Jesus of Nazareth. The Christ principle now entered the "I." Whereas in earlier times the Father principle had entered into physical body, etheric body, and astral body, now the Christ principle entered the human beings who had developed themselves to that further stage in evolution.

Now remember how I described the human being in the second lecture. I said to you that the plant nullifies within itself physical nature. One might also say that the plant corrupts physical nature. The animal then corrupts the physical and the etheric. Human beings corrupt the physical, etheric, and astral. Human beings did not corrupt them completely during the period of human development before Golgotha, but thereafter they corrupted them completely as the "I" truly entered our being fully. Of course, initiates of the ancient mysteries freed themselves entirely from physical, etheric, and astral bodies when they let the divine Father principle flow into them and, even in those days, became "I"-beings.

By entering Jesus of Nazareth, Christ nullified, through that act, not only the physical, etheric, and astral bodies, but also the "I," to the extent that it was developed in Jesus of Nazareth at that time. Living in Jesus Christ was the *higher* Christ principle, which is related to the "I" in the same way that the human "I" is related to the astral body.

The ancient initiates, in whom higher faculties of vision had developed, were still just able to perceive the Christ event. When those ancient initiates observed human beings as they were then, they found them uniting within themselves all the forces of the other beings of nature and, as it were, above and uniting them all. They saw how we can find the mineral kingdom within the human physical body, the plant kingdom in the human etheric body, the animal kingdom in the human astral body, and then they saw what is actually human. When tidings of this Christ event, of the approaching event of Golgotha, came to the initiates who had achieved clairvoyant seeing in ancient times, to these Fathers of the peoples, at least to those few who were still present—when these tidings came, these initiates could see a being in Christ in whom still more was contained, in whom not merely had earthly being been elevated to the human level but in whom humanity itself had been elevated to the level of being that is spiritual and divine.

If we bear in mind how there is present in the human being something that lives in the external physical body as an expression of essential humanity then we can understand how these initiates saw more in Jesus Christ than a mere man, how they saw walking around on the Earth something that went beyond the human, beyond humanity. These initiates saw Jesus Christ in a special radiance. They saw him covered not only with the color of human flesh but with a special shimmering radiance.

Initiates in ancient times could, of course, see this special shining radiance in their fellow initiates. It was the power of the Father principle that dwelled within them. But now they perceived not only what lived in the old initiates as the divine Father principle; now they perceived something that radiated from Jesus Christ in a special way, because not only had physical, etheric, and astral bodies been nullified in him, but also the "I" to the extent that the "I" could be present in a human being at that time.

Consequently, not just initiates but also other specially gifted people were able to see Jesus Christ as an especially radiant being. This was the radically new reality at the time of The Mystery of Golgotha—even new to the initiates—that other human beings, though perhaps few in number, who were only endowed with natural powers, not with powers otherwise acquired only in the mysteries, could recognize in Jesus Christ this higher nature.

A realization arose from this fact that now, with The Mystery of Golgotha, something was supposed to happen that, in earlier times, had taken place only within the mysteries themselves. Something that had previously taken place only within the mysteries—the microcosm, the "little world"—had been carried out into the macrocosm—the "greater world." It is actually true that, initially, the Christ mystery was proclaimed in its clearest and purest form in the last remaining mystery centers of antiquity. It was precisely this proclamation of the mystery of Christ that was lost to later civilization during the first four centuries of European development. Because not just the Father principle but also the Son principle lived in Jesus Christ, the ancient initiates recognized that he represented something absolutely unique in earthly development. It was unique in this respect: In the further advance of the Earth, never again could another Mystery of Golgotha appear; never again could such an indwelling of the Son principle in a human being take place as had occurred in Jesus of Nazareth.

And these initiates knew that Christ had entered into humanity as the healer, as the great healer, as the being who prevents the human body from suffering damage caused by the brittleness that was brought about through the entrance of the "I." For what would have happened if Christ had not appeared as the healer? If Christ had not appeared as the healer, then when human beings die, when they lay aside the decaying body, the products of this decay would radiate back into the soul being that the human being unfolds after death. The dead would have been disturbed, tortured, by what the decaying physical body represented in Earth existence. These souls who had passed through death would have been forced own "I"-consciousness. They themselves actually would not have been able to be good; it would only have been Christ in them who was good. Human beings would have had to walk about upon the Earth with the Christ dwelling within them, and inasmuch as Christ would have availed himself of the bodies of human beings, the healing of these bodies would have occurred. But the good deeds accomplished by human beings would have been the deeds of Christ, not the deeds of human beings.

That was not the task, the mission, of the divine Son, who had united himself with the evolution of the Earth through The Mystery of Golgotha. He wanted to live within humanity without clouding the dawning human "I"-consciousness. He did this once—in Jesus, in whom, from the baptism onward, the consciousness of the Son God lived in place of the "I"-consciousness of Jesus. But this was not to happen in the human beings of the times to come. In the people of future times the "I" was to be able to raise itself to full, clear consciousness, while Christ nevertheless continued to dwell within them.

For this to happen it was necessary for Christ, as such, to disappear from the immediate sight of human beings. Although he remained united with earthly existence, he disappeared from the direct view of human beings. A saying common in the ancient mystery centers became also applicable to him. In the mysteries it was said that when a physically visible being, a being whose existence can be followed by human beings with their perception in the physical world, ceases to be visible—it was said that such a being had "ascended to the heavens," and passed into those regions where physical visibility no longer exists. And so Christ ascended to heaven and became invisible. In a certain sense he would have retained his visibility if he had dwelled in human beings and eliminated the "I," so that they could have become good only because, in reality, the Christ was acting in them.

The kind of vision that enabled the apostles, the disciples, to behold Christ even after his resurrection—that kind of vision disappeared. Christ had ascended to the heavens. But he sent to human beings that divine being who does not extinguish "I"-consciousness. This is the one to whom human beings raise themselves, not through earthly perception but with imperceptible spirit. Christ sent humanity the Holy Spirit.

Actually, it is the Holy Spirit who is sent by Christ so that humans might retain their self-awareness, or "I"-consciousness, while Christ himself lives in the human unconsciousness. Thus, if human beings realize in the full sense of the word what their being really is, they will be able to look back to what the ancient initiates knew and see that living within them is the Father principle that fills the cosmos and arose in those initiates and developed the "I" within them. That is the principle living within us before we come down to the physical world. Because the Father principle lived in in them, ancient initiates remembered with complete clarity the way they lived before descending to the physical world. They sought the divine in the realm of being that precedes birth, the realm of preexistence: *Ex deo nascimur.*

After The Mystery of Golgotha, human beings could no longer "behold the Christ," otherwise they could not have become good through themselves; only Christ within could have done the good. The truth could have been only *In Christo morimur.* Human beings could die in Christ; through the principle of death within them, they could unite with Christ. But new human consciousness could be awakened through the Holy Spirit, the being sent to us by Christ: *Per spiritum sanctum reviviscimus.*

Here you have the inner connection of the Trinity, also showing something else that is definitely part of Christianity. Even without perception of Christ within, human beings can achieve awakening of the spirit. By sending the Holy Spirit, Christ gave humanity the ability to rise to an understanding of the spiritual from the life of intellect itself. Hence, it should not be said that human beings cannot grasp the spiritual, or suprasensory, through their own spirit. People could justify their inability to understand the spirit only by ignoring the Holy Spirit and speaking only of the Father God and the Christ God. For those willing to see and read, it is also clearly indicated (it is a revelation in and of itself) that humans can understand the suprasensory through the spirit dwelling within them, if they only incline themselves toward Christ. This is why we are told that the Holy Spirit appeared at the baptism of Christ. With the appearance of the Holy Spirit, these words resound through the cosmos: "This is my beloved Son; this day I have begotten him."

The Father is the unbegotten begetter who places the Son into the physical world. But at the same time the Father uses the Holy Spirit in order to tell humanity that in the spirit, the suprasensory is comprehensible, even if this spirit is itself not perceptible but only works inwardly to elevate the merely abstract intellect to the realm of the living. In the spirit the suprasensory can be understood when the corpse of thoughts that we have from our prebirth existence is raised to life through the Christ dwelling within us. And when Christ sent the Holy Spirit to his disciples—this imparting occurred through the Christ, through the Son. For this reason it was an ancient dogma that the Father is the unbegotten begetter, that the Son is the one begotten by the Father, and that the Holy Spirit is the one imparted to humanity by the Father and the Son. This is not some kind of arbitrarily asserted dogma but rather the wisdom of initiation living in the earliest Christian centuries; only later was it covered over and buried along with the teachings concerning the Trichotomy and the Trinity.

The divine principle working as Christianity within evolving humanity cannot be understood without the Trinity. If, in the place of the Trinity, some other teaching concerning God were to enter, then basically speaking it would not be a fully Christian teaching. One must understand the Father, the Son, and the Holy Spirit if one would understand the teaching concerning God concretely and in a genuine way.

The Gospel itself was no longer understood when Scholasticism decreed that human beings have revelation only in faith, that they cannot reach the suprasensory through their own human knowledge. This decree concerning human knowledge, which was separated off from faith, was itself a sin against Christianity; it was a sin against the proclamation of the Holy Spirit through the Father at the baptism of Jesus, and through Jesus himself when he sent the Holy Spirit at Pentecost.

Thus within the development of European civilization many sins were committed in what continued to call itself Christianity, many sins were committed against the original impulses of Christianity. Today it is really necessary for humanity to turn back to these original impulses of Christianity. In many ways these original Christian impulses have hardened into dogmas. But if one penetrates into the living spirit then what is essentially true in these dogmas can catch fire. Then they will cease to be dogmas. What is false in the Church is not that it has propagated the dogmas but that it has frozen and crystallized them, has taken them away from the realm of human knowledge. Because human knowledge was limited to only what is in the world of the senses the dogmas had to be crystallized, had to become no longer understandable. For it is an impossibility that faith alone could ever really bring understanding. What must be rescued within humanity is knowledge itself; knowledge must be led back to the suprasensory.

Fundamentally speaking, this challenge reaches to us from Golgotha when we rightly understand it, when we know how,

Lecture Four

after going through The Mystery of Golgotha, Christ sent into humanity, in addition to this divine Father principle, the Holy Spirit. Whoever beholds the cross on Golgotha must at the same time behold the Trinity, for in reality Christ shows and makes manifest the Trinity in all the ways he is interwoven with the earthly evolution of humanity.

This, my dear friends, is what I wanted to bring to you today, which will provide us with the basis for further studies in the future.

Part Two

The Mission of the Spirit

I

MEDITATION: THE PATH TO HIGHER KNOWLEDGE

Oxford, August 20, 1922

I would like to respond to your kind invitation to speak here this evening by telling you something about how, through unmediated research, one can come to spiritual knowledge, and I would like to explain the educational consequences of that knowledge. At the outset today, I would also like to say that I will be speaking primarily about the method for entering and researching suprasensory worlds; perhaps on another occasion it will be possible to impart some of the results of suprasensory research. Everything I have to say today will refer to *researching* spiritual, suprasensory worlds, not to *understanding* suprasensory knowledge. Suprasensory knowledge that has been researched and communicated can be understood by ordinary healthy human understanding if that understanding has not lost its unbiased perspective. A biased view is present when the understanding starts with the proof or logical deduction appropriate for dealing with the outer world of senses. Because of this hindrance alone it is often said that the results of suprasensory research cannot be understood by anyone who is not a researcher of the suprasensory.

What will be imparted here today is the object of what is known as initiation knowledge. In previous ages of humanity's development this knowledge was cultivated in a form different from the form appropriate for today. As I have said in other lectures, the things of the past are not to be brought forward again; rather the path of research into suprasensory worlds is to be entered upon in a way appropriate to the thinking and feeling of our age. When it comes to initiation knowledge, everything depends on the ability of individuals to undergo a fundamental reorientation or re-visioning of their entire soul configuration.

Individuals having initiation knowledge are distinguished from those who have knowledge in today's sense of the word, not merely because their initiation knowledge is a step above ordinary knowledge. Of course, it is achieved on the foundation of ordinary knowledge; this foundation must be present; intellectual thinking must be fully developed if we want to acquire initiation knowledge. However, a fundamental reorientation is then necessary. Those who possess initiation knowledge must come to see the world from a perspective altogether different from the way it was seen without initiation knowledge.

I can express the fundamental difference between initiate and ordinary knowledge in a simple formula: In ordinary knowledge we are aware of our thinking; indeed, we are altogether aware of the inner soul experience through which we, as the subject of knowing, acquire knowledge. For example, when we think and believe that we know something through thought we think of ourselves as thinking human beings, as subjects. We are looking for objects when we observe nature or human life or perform experiments. We always look for objects. Objects are supposed to present themselves to us. Objects should surrender themselves to us so we can encompass them with our thoughts, so we can apply our thinking to them. We are the subject and what comes to us is the object.

With those who strive for initiation knowledge, an entirely different orientation comes into play. They must become aware that, as human beings, they are the object; then, for this object, or human being, they must seek the subject. A situation exactly the opposite of ordinary knowing must occur. In ordinary knowledge we experience ourselves as subject and look for the object outside of us. In initiation knowledge we ourselves are the object, and we seek the corresponding subject; in other words, genuine initiation knowledge leads us to find subjects. But that would be the object of a later knowledge.

It is as though the mere definitional concepts already force us here to see that in initiation knowledge, we must actually flee from ourselves; we must become like the plants and stones, like thunder and lightning, which are, for us, objects. In initiation knowledge we slip out of ourselves, so to speak, and become objects that seek the corresponding subjects. If I may express myself somewhat paradoxically, I would like to say that from the point of view of thinking the difference is as follows: In ordinary knowing we think about the things; in initiation knowledge we seek to discover how *we* are being thought by the cosmos.

This is nothing more than an abstract guiding principle. But you will find that this abstract guiding principle is followed everywhere in the concrete methods of initiation. To begin with, if we want to receive initiation knowledge appropriate for today we must proceed from thinking. The life of thought must be fully developed if we want to come to initiation knowledge today. This life of thought can be especially well schooled through an immersion in the natural scientific development of the last centuries, the nineteenth century in particular.

People react in different ways to natural scientific knowledge. Some listen to the pronouncements of science with what I would like to call a certain naivete. They hear, for example, how organic beings have developed from the simplest, most primitive forms up to the human being. They think about this development but have little regard for their own involvement in these ideas. They do not stop to consider the fact that they themselves unfold something in the seeing of external processes, something that belongs to the life of thought.

However, those who receive natural scientific knowledge with critical consideration of their own involvement must ask themselves what it means that we ourselves can follow the development of beings from the imperfect to the perfect? Or one could say: When I do mathematics I create thoughts purely from myself. Properly understood, mathematics is a web spun from myself. I then apply this web to the outer world, and it fits. Here we come to the great question—I would like to say, the really tragic question: How do things stand with respect to thinking itself—this thinking that is involved every time I know something? No matter how long we think about it, we cannot discover how things stand with thinking, which always remains stuck in the same place. We merely spin, so to speak, around the axis we have already built for ourselves. We must accomplish something with our thinking. With our thinking we must do what I described as meditation in my book *How to Know Higher Worlds*.[1]

We should not think mystically about meditation but then neither should we think of it lightly. It must be completely clear what meditation is in the modern sense. It also requires patience and inner energy of soul. Above all there is something else that belongs to meditation, something that no one can ever give to another human being: the ability to promise oneself something and then keep that promise. When we begin to meditate we begin to perform the only really fully free act in human life. We always have the tendency toward freedom within us. We have also attained a good measure of freedom. However, if we stop to think about it, we will find we are dependent upon our heredity, our education, and our present life situation.

To what extent are we in a position to suddenly leave behind all we have acquired through heredity, education, and life? We would be confronted with nothingness were we to suddenly leave that all behind.

Although we may have decided to meditate mornings and evenings in order gradually to learn to see into the spiritual world, we can, in fact, on any given day, leave this undone. There is nothing to prohibit this. And experience teaches us that most people who approach the meditative life, even those with the best intentions, soon leave it again. In this we are completely free. Meditation is an essentially free act.

If we are able to remain true to ourselves despite this freedom, if we promise ourselves, not another but ourselves, that we will remain faithful to this meditation, then that is, of itself, an enormous power in the soul.

Having said that, I would like to draw your attention to how, in its simplest form, meditation is done. I can only deal with the basic principles today. This is what we are dealing with: An idea or image, or a combination thereof, is moved into the center of our consciousness. Although the content of this thought complex does not matter, it should be immediate and not represent anything from our memory. For this reason it is good if the thought complex is not retrieved from our memory but rather given to us by someone experienced in such things. It is good for it to be given to us, not because the one who gives the meditation wants to exercise any suggestion but because we then can be certain that what we meditate is, for us, something entirely new.

We could just as well find a passage for meditation in any old book that we know we have not read. What is important is that we not pull a sentence out of our subconscious or unconscious, which would then overwhelm us. We could never be absolutely certain about a sentence like that. All kinds of things left over from past feelings and sensations would be mixed in. It is essential that the meditation be as transparent as a mathematical equation.

Let us take something very simple, the sentence: "Wisdom lives in the light." To begin with, the truth of this sentence cannot be tested. It is a picture. But it is not important for us to concern ourselves with the content in any other way than to see through and understand it. We are to dwell upon it with our consciousness. In the beginning we will only be able to dwell in full consciousness upon such a content for a very short period of time. But this period of time will get longer and longer.

What then is essential? Everything depends upon our gathering together our whole life of soul in order to concentrate all our powers of thinking and feeling upon the content of the meditation. Just as the muscles of the arm become strong as we work with them, so too soul forces are strengthened by focusing them on a meditative content again and again. If possible the content of meditation should remain the same for months, perhaps for years. For genuine suprasensory research the forces of the soul must first be strengthened, empowered.

If we continue practicing in this way, the day will come, I would like to say, the big day, on which we make a very special observation. Gradually we observe that we are in a soul activity entirely independent of the body. We notice that whereas previously we were dependent upon the body for all our thinking and feeling—for our thinking upon the nervous system, for our feeling upon the circulatory system, and so on—now we feel ourselves in a spiritual-soul activity that is fully independent of any bodily activity. And we notice this because we are now in a position to cause something in our head to vibrate, something that had remained entirely unconscious previously. We now discover the strange difference between sleeping and waking. The difference is this: When we are awake, something is vibrating throughout our entire organism, except in our head. What is otherwise in movement in all the rest of the human organism is at rest in the head.

We will understand better what we are dealing with here if I point to the fact that, as human beings, we are not these robust solid bodies that we usually believe ourselves to be. We are actually made up of approximately ninety percent fluids; and the ten percent solid constituents are immersed and swimming around in the fluids. We can speak of the solid part of human beings only in an uncertain way. We are, if I may put it this way, approximately ninety percent water, and to a certain extent, air and warmth pulsate through this water.

If you can imagine the human being this way—to the least extent solid body and to a greater extent water and air with warmth vibrating therein—then you will not find it so difficult to believe that there is something even finer and more rarefied within us. This finer element I will call the etheric body. This etheric body is more rarefied than air. It is so fine that it permeates us without our being aware of the fact—at least in ordinary life. This etheric body is what is in inner movement when we are awake—in a regular movement throughout the entire human body, except in the head. In the head the etheric body is inwardly at rest.

In sleep it is otherwise. Sleep begins and then continues when the etheric body also begins to be in movement in the head. So that in sleep the whole human being—the head as well as the rest of the human being—has an etheric body that is in inner movement. When we are dreaming, for example, just upon awakening, we are then still just able to perceive the last movements of the etheric body. They present themselves to us as dreams. We are still able to perceive the last etheric movements in the head; however, when we awaken quickly that cannot happen.

Those who meditate for a long time as I have indicated reach a stage where they can form pictures in the etheric body that permeate the head when it is at rest. In *How to Know Higher Worlds,* I call these pictures *Imaginations.* Such Imaginations, which can be experienced in the etheric body, independently of the physical body, are the first suprasensory impressions we can have. They bring us to the place where, entirely without regard for our physical body, we can behold, as in *one* picture, our life in its movement and its actions. What has often been described by people who were submerged in water and about to drown—seeing their lives backward in a series of moving pictures—can be developed here systematically, so that everything that has happened in our present earthly life can be seen.

The first result of initiation knowledge is a view of our own soul life. This turns out to be entirely different from what one usually expects. We usually abstractly suppose this soul life to be woven from ideas and mental images. When we discover it in its true form we find that it is something creative and, at the same time, that it is what was working in our childhood, what shaped and molded our brain, what permeates the rest of the body and brings about a plastic form-building activity within the body as it enkindles and supports our waking consciousness, even our digestive activity. We see this inner activity in the organism as the etheric body of the human being. This is not a spatial body but a time body. For this reason you can describe the etheric body as a form in space only if you realize that what you are doing is the same as painting a bolt of lightning. When you paint a picture of a lightning flash you are, of course, painting only a moment of its existence. You are holding the moment in place. The human etheric body also can only be captured as a spatial form for a moment. In reality we have a physical body in space and an etheric body in time, a time body, which is always in movement. And it is only meaningful to speak of the etheric body if we speak of it as a body of time that we can behold. From the moment we are in a position to make this discovery we see it extending backward all the way back to our birth. This is, to begin with, the first suprasensory ability we can discover in ourselves.

The development of the soul, brought about through processes such as I have described, shows itself above all in a change of the entire soul mood and disposition of those people who strive for initiation knowledge. Please do not misunderstand me; I do not mean that someone who arrives at initiation knowledge suddenly becomes an entirely transformed and different person. On the contrary, modern initiation knowledge must leave us standing fully in the world, so that we are able to continue our life, when we return to it, just as we once began it. But when suprasensory research is carried out, through initiation knowledge during those hours and moments, we become different from what we are in ordinary life.

Above all, I would like to emphasize an important moment that characterizes initiation knowledge. As we penetrate further into experience of the suprasensory, we feel increasingly how our own bodily nature disappears—that is, it disappears for us with respect to the activities in which our bodily nature plays a part in ordinary life.

Let us consider for a moment how our judgments in life come about. We grow up and develop as children. Sympathy and antipathy become solidly set in our lives—sympathy and antipathy for the things that appear to us in nature and for other people. Our body is involved in all of this. Of course, this sympathy and antipathy that, to a large extent, actually have their foundation in the physical processes in our body, are then placed and located in the body. In the moment when people about to be initiated rise into the suprasensory world, they live into a world in which, for the duration of the time spent in the suprasensory, the sympathies and antipathies connected with their bodily nature become increasingly foreign to them. They are lifted above that with which their bodily nature is connected. When they wish to take up ordinary life again they must again fit themselves, so to speak, into their usual sympathies and antipathies—something that otherwise occurs by itself.

When we awaken in the morning we fit into our bodies, develop the same love for things and people, the same sympathy and antipathy we had before. This happens by itself. But when we stay for a while in the suprasensory and then wish to return to our sympathies and antipathies, then we must exert an effort to submerge ourselves into our bodily nature. This condition of separation from our own bodily nature is a phenomenon that shows that we are really making progress. The appearance of wide-hearted sympathies and antipathies is, altogether, something that initiates gradually make a part of their being.

There is one thing that shows the development toward initiation in a particularly strong way: the working of the memory during initiation knowledge. We experience ourselves in ordinary life. Our memory is sometimes a little better, sometimes a little worse; but we acquire a memory. We have experiences and later remember them. This is not the case with what we experience in suprasensory worlds. We can experience greatness, beauty, and meaning, but after it has been experienced it is gone. And it must be experienced again if it is to stand before the soul again. It is not imprinted in the memory in the usual sense. It is imprinted only if we bring into concepts what we have seen in the suprasensory, only if we can also bring our understanding along with us into the suprasensory world. This is very difficult. We must be able to think just as well on the other side but without the body helping with this thinking. For this reason our concepts must be strengthened beforehand; we must have become proper logicians before, so that we do not always forget when we look into the suprasensory world. It is just the primitive clairvoyants who, although they can see quite a bit, forget their logic when they are over there. It is just when we want to share suprasensory truths with someone else that we notice this change in our memory with respect to these truths. From this we can see how our physical body is involved in the exercise of memory, not in thinking, but in the exercise of memory, which always plays into the suprasensory.

If I may say something personal, it is this: When I myself hold lectures, it is different from the way lectures are usually held. People often speak from memory; they often develop what they have learned and thought from memory. Those who really present suprasensory truths, in fact, must always produce them in the moment when they presents them. I can hold the same lecture thirty, forty, fifty times, and for me it is never the same. Of course, that would be so in any case, but it is even more so with this independence from memory that comes into play when we reach a higher stage of memory.

I have told you about the ability to bring forms into the etheric body of the head. This then makes it possible to see through the time-body, the etheric body, all the way back to birth. It also brings the soul to a very special mood with respect to the cosmos. One loses one's own bodily nature, so to speak, but feels oneself living into the cosmos. Consciousness expands, as it were, into the widths of the ether. One can no longer look at a plant without becoming immersed in its growth. One follows it from the root to the blossom. One lives in its juices, in its blossoms, in its fruits. One can steep oneself in the life of animals according to their forms, but especially in the life of other human beings. The slightest gesture encountered in another human being leads one, so to speak, into the entire soul life of the other person. We feel as though we are no longer in ourselves but are out of ourselves during this suprasensory knowing.

It is necessary, however, that we are able to return again and again, otherwise we are lazy, nebulous mystics, dreamers, and ignorant of suprasensory worlds. We must be able to live in suprasensory worlds while simultaneously being able to return at any time to stand firmly on our two feet. For this reason, whenever I explain such things about suprasensory worlds, I must stress that it is far more important for philosophers to know how a shoe or a coat is made than it is to know logic; they must really be in life in a practical way. Actually, people should not think about life unless they really exist in it in a practical way. This is even truer for those seeking suprasensory knowledge. Those who know the suprasensory cannot be dreamers, fanatics, or people who cannot stand on their own two feet; otherwise they would lose themselves, because we must, as a matter of fact, get outside of ourselves. But this "getting outside of ourselves" must not lead to the loss of our self. The book *An Outline of Esoteric Science* was written from such knowledge as I have described here.

Then it is important that we penetrate further into this suprasensory knowledge. This happens when we further develop our meditations. With our meditations we rest upon certain ideas or mental pictures or a combination thereof, thereby strengthening the soul life. But this is not enough to bring us fully into the spiritual world. It is also necessary that we practice the following: Beyond dwelling with our meditations upon ideas, beyond concentrating our entire soul upon these ideas, we must be able, at will, to cast them out of our consciousness. Just as, in the life of the senses, we can look at something and then away from it whenever we want, so too, in the development of suprasensory knowledge we must learn to concentrate on a content of soul and then be able to cast it out of the soul again.

Even in ordinary life this is not easy. Just think how little we have it in our power to drive our thoughts away at will. Sometimes they will pursue us for days, especially if they are unpleasant. We cannot get rid of them. This becomes much harder after we have become accustomed to concentrating on the thoughts. A thought content we have concentrated upon eventually begins to get a firm grip on us; then we really have to work hard to remove it. When we have practiced for a long time we can manage the following: We can remove, we can cast out of our consciousness, this entire retrospect of our life from birth onward, this entire etheric body, as I have called it, this time body.

This is, of course, a stage to which we must develop ourselves. We must first become mature for this step by ridding ourselves of this colossus, this giant being in our soul. The whole terrible specter that embodies life between the present moment and our birth is standing there before us. This is what we must do away with. If we can get rid of it then something will appear for us that I would like to call a *more wakeful* consciousness. Then we are merely awake without anything in the waking consciousness. Then it begins to fill. Just as air streams into lungs that need it, so too the real spiritual world now streams into the consciousness that has been emptied in the way described.

This is Inspiration. Now something streams in that is not a finer, more rarefied matter. It is related to matter as negative is related to positive. The *opposite* of matter now streams into the human being who has become free of the ether. This is the most important thing we can become aware of. It is not true that spirit is merely an even finer, more etherealized form of matter. If we call matter the positive (it really does not matter if we call it positive or negative; these things are relative), then in terms of the positive we must call spirit negative. It is as if I had the vast fortune of five dollars in my wallet. If I give one away then I will have four left. But say, alternatively, that I accumulate debts. If I owe one dollar then I have less than no dollars.

If through the methods described I have removed the etheric body then I come, not into a still finer ether, but into something that is the opposite of ether, in the same way debts are the opposite of assets. Now I know from my own experience what spirit is. Through Inspiration the spirit comes into us and the first thing we experience is what surrounded our soul and spirit before our birth, that is before conception, in the spiritual world. That is, the preexistent life of our soul and spirit. Previously we had seen into the etheric realm back to our birth. Now we look back beyond birth, that is conception, into a world of soul and spirit and reach the point where we can perceive how we were before we descended from spiritual worlds into a physical body taking on a line of heredity.

For Inspiration knowledge these things are not thought-out philosophical truth. They are experiences, but experiences that must only be acquired after a preparation such as I have indicated. So the first thing that comes to us when we enter the spiritual world is the truth of the preexistence of the human soul, that is, of the human spirit. We learn now to see the eternal directly.

For many centuries now European humanity has considered eternity from one side only, from the point of view of immortality. Europeans have asked only: What becomes of the soul after it leaves the body at death? Of course, it is the egotistical right of human beings to ask such a question. They are interested in what will follow after death for egotistical reasons. We will presently see that we too can speak about immortality, but immortality is usually discussed for egotistical reasons. People are less interested in what happened before their birth. They say:

We are *here* now. What went on before has value only as history. But knowledge of history that has any value is only possible if we seek knowledge of our existence before birth, that is, before conception.

We need a word in modern languages that makes the eternal complete. We should speak not only of immortality but also of *unbornness*. For eternity consists of both immortality and unbornness; furthermore, initiation knowledge discovers unbornness before it discovers immortality.

A further stage of development in the direction of the spiritual world can be reached if we strive to free our soul and spiritual activities still further from the support given by the body. We can achieve this freeing by guiding our exercises, meditations, and concentration more in the direction of will-exercises. As a concrete example I would like to describe a simple will exercise that will allow you to study the principle under consideration. In ordinary life we are accustomed to think along with the flow of the world. We let the things come to us as they happen to come. What comes to us first we think first, what comes to us later we think later. And even if in more logical thinking we are not thinking along with the flow of time, still in the background there is the effort to stick with the external, "real," flow of events and facts. To exercise our soul and spiritual forces we must get free from the external flow of events. And a good will exercise is this: We try to think back through the experiences of the day, not as they occurred, from the morning to evening, but backward, from evening to morning, paying attention to the details as much as possible.

Suppose we come to the following in this backward review: We walked up a set of stairs. First we picture ourselves on the top step, then at the one before the top, and so on down to the bottom. We descend the stairs backward. In the beginning we will only be able to visualize backward the episodes of the day's experiences in this way, say from six o'clock to three o'clock, or from twelve to nine, and so on, back to the moment of waking. But gradually we will acquire a kind of technique by means of which, as a matter of fact, in the evening or the next morning we will be able to let a tableau of the day's events, or the events of the day before, pass before our soul in reverse order.

When we are in a position (and everything depends on our achieving this position) to free ourselves entirely from the three dimensional flow of reality, then we will see how a powerful strengthening of our will occurs. The same effect can be achieved if we are able to hear a melody backward or if we can picture a drama of five acts running backward from the fifth, fourth, and so on back to the first. We strengthen our will inwardly with all of these means, and outwardly we tear it free from its bondage to events in the world of the senses. Other exercises that I have mentioned in previous lectures can be added. We can take stock of ourselves and our habits. We can take ourselves in hand, apply iron will in order, in a few years, to acquire another habit in place of the old. As an example, I mention the fact that in his handwriting everyone has something that reveals his character. Making the effort to acquire another handwriting, one that is not at all similar to the former, requires a powerful, inner strength. Of course, the second handwriting must become just as habitual as the first. That is a small thing. There are many such things through which we can alter the fundamental direction of our will through our own energetic efforts.

In this way gradually we are able to do more than just bring the spiritual world as Inspiration into us. With our spirit freed from the body we are really able to immerse ourselves in the other spiritual beings outside us. Genuine spiritual knowing means that we enter into spiritual beings around us when we behold physical things. If we want to know spiritual things we must first get out of ourselves. I have described this freeing of ourselves from the physical. But then we must also acquire the ability to sink ourselves again into spiritual things and beings.

We can only do this after practicing the kinds of exercises just described; then, as a matter of fact, we are no longer disturbed by our own bodies but can immerse ourselves in the spiritual side of things; then the plants no longer merely appear to us, but we are able to dive down into the color itself. We live in the process whereby the plant colors itself. By not only knowing that the chicory growing alongside the road is blue, but by being able to enter into the blossom inwardly and participate in the blue we dwell intuitively in this process. From this point we can extend our knowledge more and more.

From certain symptoms we can tell we have really made progress with such exercises. I would like to mention two, but there are really many. The first symptom involves this—that we acquire views of the world of morality entirely different from those we had before. For the pure intellect the moral world is something unreal. Certainly, if we have remained decent people during the age of materialism, we feel obligated to do what the old traditions prescribe. Yet, even if we do not admit it, we think to ourselves that doing the good does not make something happen that is as real as lightning flashes or thunder rolling through space. We are not thinking of reality in this sense when we consider morality. But when we live into the spiritual world, we realize that the moral order of the world not only has a reality such as we find in the physical world but is actually a higher reality.

We gradually come to understand that this entire age, with its physical ingredients and processes, can decay and be dissolved; but the morality that flows from our actions continues to exist through its effects. We become aware of the reality of the moral world. The physical and moral worlds, being and becoming are then one. We really experience the truth that moral laws are also objective laws of the world.

This experience intensifies our sense of responsibility toward the world. It gives us a completely different consciousness, one much needed by modern humanity. Modern humanity looks at the beginning of the Earth—how it was formed from a primal plasma in space; how life, humankind, and, much like a *fata morgana,* the world of ideas arose from this primal matter. Our present-day humanity looks at the cold grave of the universe that entropy will bring us to. According to this materialistic idea, everything in which human beings live will again sink into a great graveyard. Humanity needs knowledge of the moral order in the world, the knowledge that can be achieved through suprasensory sources. This I can only touch on in this lecture.

Another symptom of our progress must be mentioned: the intensified suffering that we experience. We cannot come to intuitive knowledge, to this submerging of ourselves in things external to ourselves, without having gone through an intensified suffering. This suffering is intensified compared with the pain involved in imaginative knowledge, the pain that always arises when we must find our way again into our sympathies and antipathies. The great effort required to find our way back always hurts. The pain now becomes a cosmic mutual experience of all the suffering that rests upon the ground of existence.

It is easy to ask why the gods, or God, created suffering. Suffering must exist if the world is to arise in its beauty. We have eyes because, to begin with, in a still undifferentiated organism something organic was, so to speak, "dug out" and transformed into the power to see and, then, into the eye. If we were still able today to perceive the tiny, insignificant processes that go on in the retina when we see, then we could perceive that even those processes represent a pain that rests upon the ground of existence. All beauty rests on the foundation of suffering. Beauty can only be developed out of pain. We should be able to feel this pain, this suffering. We can only really find our way into the spiritual by going through pain. To a lesser degree this can already be said for a lower stage of knowledge. Anyone who has acquired even a little knowledge will admit to the following: I am grateful to my destiny for the happiness and joys life has brought me, but my knowledge has only been achieved through my pains, through my suffering.

If this is felt with respect to more elementary knowledge, it can then become an even greater experience when we overcome ourselves, when we find our way through the pain that is felt as cosmic pain to a neutral experience in the spiritual cosmos. We must struggle through to jointly experiencing the events and essential nature of all things; then intuitive knowledge is present. We are fully within an experience of knowledge that is no longer bound to the body. We can then return to and live again in the sensible world until death but with full knowledge of what it means to be real, to be real in the soul-spiritual outside the body.

If we grasp this experience of intuitive knowledge, then, in a picture, we have knowledge of what happens when we leave the physical body at death, then we know what it means to go through the gate of death. The reality we encounter, that the soul and spirit go over into a world of soul and spirit when they leave the body behind—we experience this reality beforehand when we have ascended to intuitive knowledge. That is, we know what it is like in a world where there is no body to provide support. When we have then brought this knowledge into concepts, we return to the body. But the essential thing is that we learn how to live without a body and acquire thereby the knowledge of what it will be like when we can no longer use our body, when we lay it aside at death and step over into a world of soul and spirit. Once again, this is not a question of philosophical speculation concerning immortality based upon initiation knowledge. It is, I would like to say, an experience, a pre-experience of what is to come. We know what it will be like. We do not experience the full reality of dying, but we experience immortality. This experience also becomes a part of our knowledge.

I have attempted to describe how you can rise through Imagination, Inspiration, and Intuition and how, through this development, you can learn to know yourself in your full reality as a human being. In the body we learn to know ourselves for as long as we are in the body. But we must free our soul and spirit from the body, for only then can the whole human being be free. What we know through the body, through our senses, through thinking based on sense experience and bound up with the body's nervous system—with all this we can know only one part of us. We only learn to know the whole human being if we have the will to ascend to the knowledge that comes from initiation science.

Once again, I would like to stress that once the research has been done, then the results can be understood—just as what astronomers and biologists say about the world can be understood and tested—by anyone approaching them with an unprejudiced mind, with ordinary, healthy human understanding. Then you will find that this testing is the first step of initiation knowledge. Because people do not seek untruth and error but truth, we must first get an impression of the truth in initiation knowledge. Then, as much as destiny makes it possible for us, we will be able to penetrate the spiritual world further and further.

In our day, in a higher sense, the words inscribed above the Greek temple as a challenge must be fulfilled: "Human being, know yourself."

Those words certainly did not mean that we should retreat into our inner life. They were, rather, a challenge to search for our being: to search for the essence of immortality, which is found in the body, to search for the essence of unbornness, which is found in the immortal spirit, and to search for the mediator between Earth, time, and spirit that is the soul. For the true human being consists of body, soul, and spirit. The body can know only the body, the soul can know only the soul, and spirit can know only the spirit. Therefore, we must try to find the spirit active within us so that the spirit can also be recognized in the world.

2

The Cosmic Origin of the Human Form

The Need to Return to the Spiritual Life

Oxford, August 22, 1922

Today we would like to look at some things that will bring together for a wider circle of anthroposophists many of the truths already known to us. Perhaps you are already familiar with the description I have given in my book *Theosophy*.[1] I described there the worlds that the human being has to live through between death and a new birth. Today I will describe something of these worlds from a point of view somewhat different from the one given in that book.

For the most part in that book Imaginations are used for the soul and spiritual worlds through which a human being passes—after going through the gate of death—in order to develop and advance to a new life on Earth. Today I will describe these things not so much from an Imaginative point of view, but rather from a point of view resulting more from Inspiration.

In order to acquire the possibility of understanding at all, we can begin with the experiences we have during earthly life. At any given point in time between birth and death we stand here in our physical body confronted with the outer world. What is contained within our skin, what is contained within our physical bodies, we call ourselves, our human being. We assume that this human being contains not only anatomical and physiological processes, but we also assume that somehow soul and spiritual processes are going on in there. We speak of "ourselves" and mean thereby what is contained within our skin. We look out into the world and see it around us; this we call our "outer world." Now, we know that we make mental pictures of this outer world and then these mental pictures live within us. We have, then, the outer world around us and something like mirror images of the outer world within our soul life.

When we are in the life between death and a new birth we are in the very same world that is outside of us here on Earth. All that you can see clearly, or only dimly sense, as an external world, becomes then your inner world. To all that you then say "my 'I.'" Just as you now regard your lung as belonging to your "I," so do you regard—in the life between death and a new birth—the Sun and Moon as your organs, as being *in* you. And the only outer world that you then have, is you yourself, as you are on the Earth, that is, your earthly organs.

While on the Earth we say that in us is a lung; in us is a heart; outside us is a Sun; outside us is a Moon; outside us is a zodiac. But during the life between death and a new birth we say that in us is a zodiac; in us is the Sun; in us is the Moon; outside us is a lung; outside us is a heart. Between death and a new birth everything we now carry within our skin becomes increasingly our outer world, our universe, our cosmos. Our view of the relationship between world and humankind is exactly opposite when we are living between death and a new birth.

So it is that when we live through death, that is, when we go through the gate of death, we have, to begin with, a distinct picture of what was before, of how we were on Earth. But it is only a picture. Yet you must think of this picture as having an effect on you like the outer world. At first you have this picture like a kind of appearance within you. In the first period after death, you still have a consciousness of what you were on Earth as a human being—consciousness in the form of earthly memories and earthly pictures. These do not last long; in your view of the human being you advance more and more to the following: I is the world; the universe is the human being. This is more and more the case. But you must not imagine that the human lung, for instance, looks the same as it does now; that would not be a sight to compensate for the beauty of the Sun and the Moon. What the lung and heart will be then is something much greater, something much more wonderful than what the Sun and Moon are now to the human eye.

Only in this way do you really get an impression of what maya is. People speak of maya, that this present earthly world is a great illusion, but they do not really believe it. Deep down people still believe that everything is just as it appears to earthly eyes. But that is not the case. The human lung as we see it now is mere semblance; so is the heart. The truth is that our lung is only a magnificent part of our cosmos, our heart even more so. For in its true essence our heart is something much more majestic, something vastly greater than any Sun.

We gradually begin to see a grand cosmic world arising—a world in which we can say that below us are the heavens. What we actually mean is that what is preparing the human head for the next incarnation is below us. Above, we then say, is what was below. Everything is turned around. Above are all the forces that prepare a human being for the earthly life, so that in his next Earth life one can stand and walk on two legs.

All this we can then sum up in these words: The closer we approach to a new life on Earth, the more this universe that is the human being contracts for us. We become increasingly aware of how this majestic universe—it is most especially majestic in the

The Cosmic Origin of the Human Form

middle period between death and a new birth—how this majestic universe, so to speak is shrinking and contracting, how, out of the weaving of the planets that we bear within us, something is created that then pulsates and surges through the human etheric body, how out of the fixed stars of the zodiac something is formed that builds our life of nerves and senses. This all shrinks together, it shapes itself to become first a spiritual and then an etheric body. And not until it has grown very, very small is it taken up into the mother's womb and clothed there with earthly matter.

Then comes the moment when we draw near to earthly life, when we feel the universe that was "ours" until recently vanishing from us. It shrinks together and becomes smaller. This experience begets in us the longing to come down again to Earth and once more unite with a physical body. We long for the Earth because this universe is withdrawing from our spiritual sight. We look to where we are becoming a human being.

However, we must reckon here with a very different scale of time. Life between death and rebirth lasts for many centuries. For those born in the twentieth century, their descent has been prepared gradually, even as early as the sixteenth century. And those individuals themselves have been working down into the earthly conditions and events.

A great, great...grandfather of yours, way back in the sixteenth century, fell in love with a great, great...grandmother. They felt the urge to come together, and there, in this urge, you were already working into the earthly world from spiritual worlds. And in the seventeenth century when a closer great, great... grandfather and great, great...grandmother loved each other, you were, in a sense, once again the mediator. You summoned all these generations together so that, finally, those who could become your mother and father could emerge.

In the mysterious and indeterminate aspect of such earthly love relationships, forces are at work that proceed from human souls seeking future incarnations. Therefore full consciousness and complete freedom are never present in the external conditions that bring men and women together. These are things that still lie entirely outside the range of human understanding.

What we call history today is actually only something very external. Little is known to us in outer life today of the soul history of human beings. People today are completely unaware that the souls of human beings even in the twelfth or thirteenth century AD felt very different from the way they do now. Not as distinctly as I have just described but in a more dreamlike way, the men and women in the tenth, eleventh, and twelfth centuries knew of these mysterious forces working down to Earth from spiritual worlds, working down, in effect, from human souls. In the West little was said about repeated earthly lives, about reincarnation, but there were human beings everywhere who knew about it. Only the churches always excluded or even anathematized all thoughts concerning repeated Earth lives. But you should actually know that there were many people in Europe, even into the twelfth and thirteenth centuries, who were aware that a human being passes through repeated lives on Earth.

Then came the time during which humanity in the Western world had to develop through the stage of intellectuality. Humankind must gradually achieve freedom. There was no freedom in ancient times when dreamlike clairvoyance prevailed. Neither is there freedom—there is, at most, belief in freedom—in those affairs of human life, governed, shall we say, by earthly love such as I have just described. For here the interests of other souls on their way down to Earth are always in play.

Yet within the course of Earth evolution humankind must grow freer and freer. Only if humankind becomes increasingly free will the Earth reach its evolutionary goal. For this to happen it was necessary that intellectuality reign in a certain age. The age in question is, of course, our own. For if you look back into earlier times and conditions upon Earth when human beings still had a dreamlike clairvoyance, you will see that spiritual beings were always living in this dreamlike clairvoyance. A person at that time could never say, "I have my thoughts in my head." That would have been quite false. In ancient times one had to say, "I have the life of angels in my head"; and then in later times one had to say "I have the life of the spirits of elemental beings in my head." Then came the fifteenth century; and in the nineteenth and the twentieth centuries we no longer have anything spiritual in our heads; only thoughts are in our heads—mere thoughts. By not having any higher spiritual life but only thoughts in our heads, we can make pictures of the outer world for ourselves. Through the fact that we no longer have any kind of higher spirituality within ourselves, but only thoughts, we are able to form pictures of the external world within ourselves.

Could human beings be free, so long as spirits were indwelling them? No, they could not. For spirits directed them in everything; everything was owed to them. We could only become free when spiritual beings no longer directed us—when we had mere pictures, mere images, in our thoughts. Thought pictures cannot compel one to do anything. If you stand in front of a mirror the reflections of other people, no matter how angry they may be, will never be able to give you a box on the ears, never a real box on the ear because they have no reality; they are mere pictures. If I decide to do something, I can arrange for this to be reflected in a mirror but the reflection itself, the picture, cannot decide on anything.

In the age when intellectuality puts only thoughts into our heads, freedom can arise because thoughts have no power to compel. If we allow our moral impulses to be only pure thoughts—as described in my book, *Intuitive Thinking as a Spiritual Path: A Philosophy of Freedom*—then we can achieve true freedom in our age.[2] The intellectual age, therefore, had to arise.

Yet strange as it may sound, in essence the time is already past in which it was right for us to develop mere intellectuality, mere thinking in pictures. Along with the nineteenth century, that has become a thing of the past. If we now continue to develop mere thoughts as images then our thoughts will fall prey to Ahrimanic powers. The Ahrimanic powers will then find access to us and, having just reached our freedom, we will lose it—lose it to Ahrimanic powers. Humanity is confronted with this danger right now. Human beings today are faced with the choice: either to comprehend the spiritual life—to understand that the kinds of things I have described to you today are realities—or to deny this. But if we deny the spiritual today we will no longer be able to think freely. Rather Ahriman, Ahrimanic powers, will then begin to think in humankind. And then all humanity will undergo a downhill evolution.

Therefore, in the highest degree, it is necessary that an increasing number of human beings in our time understand the need to return to the spiritual life. This feeling that we must return to a spiritual life is what people today should seek to awaken within themselves. If they fail to seek this, humanity will fall prey to Ahriman. Seen from a higher standpoint, this is how serious the situation of humankind on Earth is today. We should actually put this thought before all others. All other thoughts should be seen in the light of this one. This is what I wanted to present as the first part of today's lecture.

Descriptions such as these may help illustrate the fact that the life we go through in the spiritual world between death and new birth is entirely different from what we go through here between birth and death. Therefore, pictures taken from the earthly life, however brilliantly conceived, will always be inadequate to characterize the actual spiritual life of the human being. We can only slowly and gradually be led to an understanding of the kind of reality present in spiritual worlds. Let me give some examples.

Human beings leave their earthly bodies and, with their life of soul and spirit, enter the world of soul and spirit. Let us suppose that someone here on Earth who has achieved initiation knowledge in the deeper sense is able to observe human souls in their continued life after death. Much preparation is needed for this to happen; also needed is a certain karma that connects the human being on Earth with the one on the other side. The important thing is that we find some means of mutual understanding with the deceased. I am speaking to you here of spiritual experiences that are extraordinarily difficult to achieve. In general, it is easier to describe the world spiritually than to approach a departed soul. People like to believe that it is not very difficult to approach a deceased person, but it is actually far more difficult actually to approach the dead than it is to achieve spiritual knowledge in general.

I would like now to relate some features characteristic of communication with the dead. To begin with, it is only possible to communicate with them by entertaining memories of the physical world that can still live within them. For example, the dead still have an echo of human speech, even of the particular language that they spoke most of the time while on Earth. But their relationship to language undergoes a change. So, for example, when conversing with a soul who has died, we soon notice they have no understanding, not the least, for nouns. The living can address such words to a dead person; a dead person, if I may use the term, simply does not hear them. On the other hand the dead retain an understanding for all verbs, words expressing action, for a relatively long time after death.

As a general rule, you will be able to converse with a deceased person only if you know the right way to ask your questions. With these questions you must sometimes proceed as follows. One day you try to live with that individual in something concrete and real, since such individuals have pictures in their souls rather than abstract thoughts. Therefore you must concentrate on a real, concrete experience that this soul very much enjoyed during earthly life; then you can gradually approach.

As a rule you will not get an immediate answer. Often you will have to sleep on it, perhaps for several days, before you get the answer. But you will never get an answer from the dead if the question is posed in nouns. You must try to clothe all nouns in verbal form. Such preparation is absolutely necessary. What the deceased understands most readily are verbs made as pictorial and vivid as possible. The deceased will never understand for example, the word *table,* but if you manage to imagine vividly what is happening when a table is being made, which is a process of becoming rather than the finished thing, you will gradually become intelligible to that one. The deceased will understand your question and you will get an answer. But the answers, too, will always be in verbal form, or often not even in verbal form; they may consist only of what we on Earth would call interjections, exclamations.

Above all, the dead speak in the actual *sounds* of the alphabet—sounds and combinations of sound. The longer souls have lived in the spiritual world after death, the more they will come to speak in a kind of language that we on the Earth must first acquire. We do this when we develop the ability to understand and distinguish the sounds of earthly language, when we go beyond the abstract meaning of words and enter into the feeling

The Cosmic Origin of the Human Form

content of the sounds. It is just as I was saying in the educational lectures held here. With the sound *a* (as pronounced in *father*) we experience something like astonishment and wonder. In a certain sense we even take this sense of wonder into our soul when we not only say *a* but *ach* (*ch* pronounced as in *Loch*; *Ach* is the German equivalent of the exclamation *ah!*). *Ach* signifies *Ah*, to feel wonder, and with the sound *ch*, the sense of wonder goes right into me.

If I now put an *m* in front and say *mach* (German for *make* or *do*), the result is a kind of following of what awakened wonder in me as if it were approaching me step by step—*mmm*—until I am entirely within it. The answers of the dead often come in this kind of understanding, carried by the meaning in sounds. The dead do not speak in English; they do not speak in German or in Russian; they speak in such a way that only heart and soul can understand them—if heart and soul are connected to ears that hear. I said just now that the human heart is greater and more majestic than the Sun. Seen from the earthly point of view the heart is somewhere inside us, and if we cut it out anatomically it will not be a pretty sight. In reality, however, the heart is present in the entire human being, permeating all the other organs; it is also in the ear.

More and more we must get used to the language of the heart used by the dead, if I may so describe it. We get used to it as we gradually eliminate all nouns and noun-like forms and begin to live more in verbal forms. The dead understand words of activity and becoming for a relatively long time after death. At a later stage they understand a language that is no ordinary language. What we then receive from the dead must first be translated back into an earthly language.

Thus human beings grow from their body and increasingly into the spiritual world, as their entire life of soul becomes altogether different. And when the time approaches for human beings to come down to Earth again, they must once again change their entire life of soul. The moment then draws ever nearer when they are confronted with a great task, when they themselves must put together—first in the astral form and then in the etheric form—the whole future human being who will be standing here physically on Earth. What we do here on the Earth is external work. When our hands are at work then something happens in the external world. When we are between death and a new birth our soul is occupied with the work of putting our body together. It only seems as if we come into existence through hereditary forces. Actually we are only clothed in the outermost physical sheath through heredity. But even the forms of our organs we must develop for ourselves. I will give you an example of this, but I would like to borrow a glove for this purpose.

When a human being approaches a new earthly life, he still has the Sun and Moon within him. But gradually the Sun and Moon begin to contract together. It is as though you were to feel the lobes of your lungs shrinking together within you. In this way you feel your cosmic existence, your Sun- and Moon-organ shrinking together. Then something detaches itself from the Sun and from the Moon. Instead of having the Sun and Moon within you as before, you are confronted by a kind of copy, or image, of the Sun and Moon. Glistening and luminous, you have before you two, at first, gigantic spheres, one of which is the spiritualized Sun, the other the spiritualized Moon. One sphere is a bright and shining light, the other sphere is glimmering in its own warmth, more fiery warm, holding the light more to itself in an egotistical way.

These two spheres that separate themselves from the cosmically transformed human being—that is, from this Adam Kadmon that still exists to this day—these two spheres draw closer and closer to one another. On our way down to Earth we say: Sun and Moon are becoming one. And this is what guides and leads us through the last few generations of ancestors until finally we reach the mother who will give us birth. As the Sun and Moon draw ever closer together they guide us.

Then we see another task before us. We see, far in the distance like a single point, the human embryo that is to be. We see, like a single entity, what has become of Sun and Moon drawing near our mother. But we see a task before us, which I can describe as follows. Think of this glove as the Sun and Moon united and going before us, leading us. We know that when our cosmic consciousness has completely vanished, when we go through a darkness (this happens after conception when we become submerged in the embryo), that we will then have to turn this inside out. What is on the inside then comes to the outside. What the Sun and Moon have been you must turn inside out and then a tiny opening appears; through this you must go with your "I," and this becomes a copy, or image, of your human body upon Earth. And, actually, this is the pupil of the human eye. For what was one, again becomes two, as though two mirror images were to arise. These are the two human eyes; at first they were united, as the united Sun and Moon, and then they turned inside out.

This is the task that then confronts you, and you fulfill it unconsciously. You must turn the whole thing around and push what is on the inside outward and go through the tiny opening. Then it separates into two. In the embryonic state two physical images are formed. The physical embryonic eyes are two pictures representing what has become of Sun and Moon.

In this way we work out the formation of the several parts of the human body. We gather together what we experience as the entire universe and give to every part its destined form. Only then does what has been formed in the spirit get clothed in, and permeated by, a plastic material—matter. The matter is only taken on; but the forces that form and shape us we ourselves had to develop from the entire universe.

Say, for example, that in the time between death and a new birth we pass through the Sun while it is in the sign of Leo. (It need not be at birth; it can be farther back in time.) We do not then form the eyes that are made of the Sun and Moon—that occurs at a different time. But during this time we unite with the interior of the Sun. If we could walk in the interior of the Sun it would look very different from what contemporary physicists imagine. This physical imagination of theirs lacks even a suspicion of the truth. The interior of the Sun is not a ball of gas; it is something even less than space—a realm where space itself has been taken away. If you begin by imagining space as something extended, with pressure everywhere present within it, then you must picture the interior of the Sun as *negative space*, as space that is emptier than empty, a realm of suction. Few people have an adequate idea of what this means. Now, when you pass through there, you experience something that can be elaborated and worked upon, something that can be formed into the human heart. It is not the case that only the form of the eyes is made out of Sun and Moon; the heart form is also fashioned from the Sun. But this is only possible when the Sun also contains the forces that come from the constellation of Leo.

Thus, human beings build their entire body from constellations of the stars and their movements in the universe. The human organism is indeed a kind of copy or image of the world of stars. A large part of the work we have to do between death and new birth consists in this—that we build our body from the universe. Standing on the Earth the human being is indeed a universe, but a shrunken universe. Natural science is so naive as to suppose that the human form is produced from the physical

The Cosmic Origin of the Human Form

embryo alone. This is as naive as it would be for someone who sees the needle of a magnet pointing to the north and south magnetic poles to imagine that the forces causing it to point are only within the needle itself, not realizing that the Earth itself is a magnet. It is exactly the same when someone says that the human being comes from the embryo.

Human beings do not come from the embryo at all, but rather from the entire universe. Furthermore, the life of soul and spirit between death and a new birth consists of working with the spiritual beings on the suprasensory form of the human being. This form is created first in the astral and etheric realms, and only then shrinks and contracts to be clothed in physical matter. Human beings are really only the arena for what the universe—and they themselves with their transformed powers—achieves with the human physical body.

Thus, human beings gradually develop themselves. It begins with language, as we no longer use nouns but find our way into a special language, a more verbal form of speech. We then go on to inner sight of the starry world; then we live within the world of stars. From the starry world we then begin to separate out what we ourselves are to become in our next incarnation. This is humankind's path—from the physical through the transformation of language into the spiritual, and then back again through transforming the universe again into the human being. Only when we can understand how the soul-spiritual part of the human being—which thus loses itself in language—becomes one with the world of stars and then draws itself back from the world of stars do we understand the complete cycle of human life between death and a new birth.

These things were still clear to many people at the time when The Mystery of Golgotha took place on Earth. At that time people never thought of Jesus Christ as merely the being whom they saw developing on the Earth. They thought that Jesus Christ was formerly in the same world to which they themselves belonged during the life between death and new birth. They thought about the question: How did he descend and enter into the life of Earth? It was the Roman world that then exterminated the science of initiation. They wanted only the old dogmas to remain. In Italy in the fourth century of our era there was a special organization, a specific body of people who made every effort to insure that the old methods of initiation should not be transformed into new ones. Only the knowledge of the outer physical world should be left to human beings on Earth. Only the old dogmas could have any say concerning the suprasensory.

Gradually these old dogmas were received into the intellect as mere concepts that could no longer even be understood but only believed. So the knowledge that at one time had in fact existed was split in two—into knowledge of the earthly world and faith in another world. This faith has even shrunk to the point where, for some, it consists only of a collection of dogmas no longer understood, whereas for others it is no more than a mere basis for believing anything at all. What then is the substance of modern human belief, when people no longer hold to the dogmas of the Trinity? People believe something altogether nebulous, believing in a generalized, vague kind of spirituality.

We now need to return to a genuine perception of the spiritual, one made possible by living into the spiritual itself. That is, we need a science of initiation once again, a science that can speak to us about things such as the human eye, which we should look at with wonder, for it is actually a little world in itself. This is no mere picture or figure of speech; it is a reality for the reasons I have explained. For in the life between death and new birth this eye of ours was single, and this unity that was then turned inside out was actually a flowing together of the images of Sun and Moon.

Moreover, we have two eyes, because if we were equipped with only one, like the Cyclops, we could never develop a sense of self, or "I"-being, in an outer and visible world; we would develop it only in the inner world of feeling. Helen Keller, for example, has an inner world of feeling and ideas very different from that of other people; she is able to make herself understood only because a language has been taught to her. Without this, we would never be able to develop the idea of our "I." We reach the idea of "I" because we can lay our right hand over our left, or, more generally speaking, because we can bring any two symmetrical members together. We develop a delicate sense of "I"-being because we cross the axis of vision of our two eyes when focusing on the outer world. Just as we cross our hands, so do we cross our eyes' axes of vision whenever we look at anything.

Our eyes are two materially and one in spirit. This single spiritual eye is located behind the bridge of the nose. It is then reproduced in a twofold image—in the two outer eyes you see. By having a left and a right hand side, human beings are able to feel and be self-aware. If we were only right or only left, if we were not symmetrical beings, all our thinking and ideation would flow out into the world; we would not become self-possessed in our own "I."

By uniting the twin images of Sun and Moon into one, we are preparing ourselves for the coming incarnation. It is as though we were saying to ourselves: You must not disintegrate into the widths of the whole world. You cannot become a Sun-human and have the lunar-human there beside you. You must become a unified being. But then, so that you can also feel this oneness, this unified, single Sun-Moon human eye comes into being, and metamorphoses into the eye as we know it. For our two eyes are copies, or images, of the single, archetypal Sun-Moon human eye.

These are the things I wished to tell you today, my dear friends, about the entirely different kind of experience we have when we are in the spiritual world—so very different from our experiences in the physical. Nonetheless, the two experiences are related to each other. This relationship is such that we are turned completely inside out. Suppose you could take a man as you see him here and turn him inside out, so that his inside (the heart, for instance) would become the outer surface. He would not remain alive as a physical human being; you can believe that. But if this could be done taking hold of him in his *inmost heart* and turning him inside out like a glove, then the man would not remain a man as we see him here; he would enlarge into a universe.

If we had the faculty to concentrate in a single point within our own heart, and then able to turn ourselves inside out in spirit, we could become the world that we otherwise experience between death and a new birth. That is the secret of the inner side of human beings. We cannot be turned inside out only as we exist in the physical world. The human heart is also a world turned inside out. That is how the physical, earthly world is really connected to the spiritual world. We must get used to this "turning inside out." If we do not, we will never get the right idea of how the physical world that surrounds us here relates to the spiritual world.

3

The Mystery of Golgotha

Oxford, August 27, 1922

Human beings must return to the point where they can understand The Mystery of Golgotha with all the forces that live in the human soul. We must understand it not only from the limited standpoint of present-day civilization but in a way that allows all the forces of our human being to be united with The Mystery of Golgotha. But this will only become humanly possible if we are prepared to approach The Mystery of Golgotha once more from the point of view of spiritual science. There is no intellectual knowledge in a position to do justice to Christianity and the impulse it carries for the world; for every form of intellectual knowledge reaches only as far as our thinking life. And if we have a science that speaks only to our thinking, then we must seek the sources of our will impulses (and these are the most important for a true Christianity) within our instincts; we cannot sense them within the world where they are really present, within the spiritual world. In our present time it is essential to turn our attention to the great question for humanity: How and in what sense is The Mystery of Golgotha the meaning of the entire development of the Earth?

I would like to express what I am speaking of here in a picture that appears somewhat paradoxical. If a being were to descend to the Earth from another planet, this being—because it could not be a human being in the earthly sense—would probably find everything on the Earth unintelligible. But it is my deepest conviction, arrived at from the knowledge of Earth evolution, that such a being, even if it came from Mars or Jupiter, would be deeply moved by Leonardo da Vinci's painting *The Last Supper*. Such a being would find in this painting something that says a deeper meaning is associated with the Earth and its development. Beginning with this meaning, which encompasses The Mystery of Golgotha, a being from an entirely different world would be able to understand the Earth and everything appearing on it.

We who live in the present age have no idea how far we have gone into intellectual abstraction. For this reason we can no longer feel our way into the souls of people who lived a short while before The Mystery of Golgotha. Those human souls were entirely different from the souls of human beings today. We imagine human history as being more similar to the events and processes that happen today than it really was. But the souls of human beings have undergone a very significant development.

In the times before The Mystery of Golgotha human souls were such that all human beings, even those with only a primitive education, could see within themselves a being of soul. This soul being could be called a memory of the time the human being lived through before descending into an earthly body. Just as we today in ordinary life can remember what we have experienced since our third, fourth, or fifth year of life, in the same way the human soul in ancient times had a memory of its life before birth in the world of soul and spirit. In terms of their souls, human beings were, in a certain sense, transparent to themselves. They knew: I am a soul and I was a soul before I came down to Earth. And they also knew certain details of their life of soul and spirit before the descent to the Earth! They experienced themselves in cosmic pictures. They looked up and saw the stars not merely as abstract configurations as we see them today; they saw them in dreamlike Imaginations. They saw the whole world filled with dreamlike Imaginations. They could say: That is the last glimmer of the spiritual world from which I have come. When I descended as a soul from this spiritual world I entered a human body. Human beings of ancient times never united so intensively with the human body that they lost the ability to experience real soul life.

What did these human beings in ancient times experience? They experienced something that enabled them to say: Before I had descended to the Earth I was in a world where the Sun is not merely a heavenly body radiating light. I was in a world where the Sun was a gathering place for higher spiritual hierarchies. I lived not in a physical space but in a spiritual space, a world where the Sun sends out not merely light but radiant wisdom. I lived in a world where stars are essences of beings whose wills are manifest. And for these ancient people two distinct experiences were united with this feeling: the experience of nature and the experience of sin.

Modern humanity no longer has this natural experience of sin. For us sin lives only in a world of abstract existence; for us, sin is merely something projected upon nature from the world of moral abstractions. We cannot bring sin together with the necessity found in nature. For people in ancient times these two separate streams of existence, this duality, natural necessity on the one hand and moral necessity on the other, did not exist apart. All moral necessity was a necessity of nature; all necessity in nature was also a moral necessity.

So people in ancient times could say that we had to descend from the divine spiritual world. But in entering a human body we have actually become sick compared to the world from which we have descended. The concepts of sickness and sin were interwoven for the ancients. Here on the Earth, people felt that they had to find the power to overcome sickness within themselves. Therefore, those ancient souls increasingly came to the consciousness that we need an education that is, at the same time, healing. Education is medicine; education is therapy. Thus, shortly before The Mystery of Golgotha, we see the appearance of such figures as the *Therapeutae*, or healers. In Greece, too, spiritual life was thought of as connected with healing humanity. The Greeks felt that human beings had been healthier at the beginning of Earth's development and had evolved gradually in such a way as to distance themselves from divine-spiritual beings. It has been forgotten that this was the concept of "sickness," but this concept was widespread throughout the world where The Mystery of Golgotha was placed in history.

In ancient times human beings felt the reality of everything spiritual by looking into the past. They could say to themselves that we must look back to the time before our birth if we want to seek the spirit back in the past. That is where the spirit is. We were born from this spirit; we must find it again, but we have distanced ourselves from it.

In the past, human beings felt the spirit as the spirit of the Father, from whom they had separated. In the mystery religions, the highest initiates were those who had developed themselves inwardly, within the heart, within the soul forces; through this development, as human beings they could represent the Father in the outer world of Earth. When students of the mystery religions entered through the gates of mystery centers—those sacred places that were institutions of art, science, and religious consecration—and stood before the highest initiate, they saw this highest initiate as the representative of the Father God. The "Fathers" were higher initiates than the "Sun Heroes." The Father principle ruled before The Mystery of Golgotha.

Humanity felt how it had distanced itself more and more from the Father, the one to whom we can say, *Ex deo nascimur*. Humanity needed healing, and those who knew were expecting the healer of humanity, the healing savior, to come. Christ is no longer alive for us as the healing savior; only when we once again experience him as the world physician, as the great healer, only then will we be able to understand his true place in the world.

That was the underlying feeling that lived in human souls before The Mystery of Golgotha, a feeling for the connection with the suprasensory world of the Father. In Greece it was said: "Better to be a beggar upon Earth than a king in the realm of shadows." This saying expresses what was felt at that time; it bears witness to how deeply humanity had learned to feel the distance it had placed between its own being and the being of suprasensory worlds. At the same time a deep longing for the suprasensory lived in the souls of human beings.

But if humanity had gone on evolving with a consciousness only of the Father God it could never have come to full consciousness of self, of the "I," it could never have come to inner freedom. In order to come to inner freedom something that could only be seen as a sickness had to make a place for itself in the human being. It was a sickness compared to humanity's former, pristine condition. In a sense, all humanity was suffering from the Lazarus sickness. The sickness was not unto death but rather for liberation and for a new knowledge of the eternal in the human being. We can say that human beings had increasingly forgotten their past life of soul and spirit. Their attention was directed more and more to the physical world around them. When souls in ancient times looked out through the body into the physical world surrounding them, they saw, in the stars, pictures of spiritual beings they had left behind when they descended to this life through birth. They saw in sunlight the radiant wisdom that had been like an atmosphere for them in the spiritual world, an atmosphere in which they had lived and breathed. They saw in the Sun itself choirs of the higher hierarchies from which they had been sent down to Earth. But humanity came to forget all that.

And that is what people were experiencing as The Mystery of Golgotha approached in the eighth and the seventh and the following centuries before Christ's appearance on Earth. If external history says nothing of this, that is simply a failing of external history. One who can follow history with spiritual insight can see that a mighty consciousness of the Father God was present at the outset of the evolution of humanity, that this consciousness was gradually paralyzed, and that, with time, humanity was gradually supposed to see around it only nature without spirit.

Much of this process remained unspoken at the time, much was in the unconscious depths of the human soul. However, what was most of all at work in unconscious realms of the human soul was a question that was not so much expressed in words as felt in the heart: Around us is the world of nature but where is the spirit whose children we are? Where can we see the spirit whose children we are? This question lived in the best souls of the fourth, third, second, and first centuries before Christ without being consciously formulated. It was a time of questioning, a time when humanity felt distanced from the Father God. In the depths of their souls people felt: It must be true—*Ex deo nascimur!* But do we still know it? Can we still know it?

If we look even deeper into the souls of those people living at the time when The Mystery of Golgotha was approaching we see the following. There were the simpler, more primitive souls who were able only to feel deep within their unconscious life how they were now separated from the Father God. They were the descendants of primeval humanity, which was in no way as animal-like as natural science today imagines. These primitive human beings carried within their animal-like form a soul that enabled them, in an ancient dreamlike clairvoyance, to know this: We have descended from a divine-spiritual world and have taken on a human body. The Father God has led us into the world of Earth. We are born out of him.

But the oldest souls of humanity knew they had left something behind in the spiritual worlds from which they had just descended. What they left behind was afterward called, and we now call: the Christ. For this reason the earliest Christian writers maintained that the most ancient souls had been Christian; they also had known how to worship Christ. In the spiritual worlds where they had lived before descending to the Earth Christ was the center of their attention. He was the central being, toward which they directed the vision of their souls. The people on Earth remembered being together with Christ in their pre-earthly existence.

Then there were other regions (Plato speaks of them in a very special way) in which students were initiated into the mystery religions, in which vision of the suprasensory world was awakened, in which forces were released from human beings that allowed them to see into the spiritual worlds. Nor was it only in dim memory that students of the initiates came to know the Christ, the one with whom all human beings lived before their descent to Earth. In the mysteries, students came to know Christ again in his full stature. But they knew him as a being who had lost his mission, as it were, in the worlds above the Earth.

In the mystery religions of the second and third centuries before The Mystery of Golgotha initiates looked, in a very special way, to that being in the suprasensory worlds, who was later called the Christ. In looking at him they said: We see this being in the worlds above Earth but his activity in those worlds has become less and less. This is the being who had planted into human souls memories of the time before birth, memories that then came alive in earthly existence. In suprasensory worlds this being was the great teacher for what the soul could still remember after having descended to the Earth. The being who was later called Christ appeared to the initiates as a being who had lost his mission. This was because human beings gradually could no longer have, could no longer even receive, these memories.

As the initiates lived on, the consciousness arose in them more and more: This being, whom primeval humanity could remember during its life on Earth, this being, whom we see having an ever lessening amount of activity in spiritual worlds, will have to seek a new sphere of life. He will descend to the Earth to awaken suprasensory spirituality in humanity again.

And they began to speak of that being later known as Christ as the one who in the future would come down to Earth and take on a human body—as he later took on a body in Jesus of Nazareth. Speaking of the Christ as the one who is to come formed the chief content of much of their teaching in the last centuries before The Mystery of Golgotha. In the beautiful and powerful picture of the wise men from the East, the three kings or magi, we see representatives of the initiates who in their places of initiation had learned: the Christ will come when the time has been fulfilled; signs in the heavens will proclaim his coming. Then we must seek him at his hidden place. A deeper secret, a deeper mystery can be heard sounding through the Gospels. When the evolution of humanity is looked at with spiritual vision this deeper mystery is revealed.

Primitive human beings looked up, as if lost, to the suprasensory. In their unconscious they said to themselves: We have

The Mystery of Golgotha

forgotten Christ. They saw the world of nature around them and the question rose in their hearts: How can we again find the suprasensory world? And the initiate in the mysteries knew: This being, who will later be called the Christ, will come and take on human form; what human souls had formerly experienced in their pre-earthly existence they will then experience in looking upon The Mystery of Golgotha.

Thus, through the mighty fact of the greatest event ever to take place on Earth—not in an abstract intellectual fashion—answer is given to the question: How can we again come to higher worlds that transcend the world of sense? The people of that time who had developed a feeling for what had happened, these people learned from those who knew that a real God dwelt in the human being Jesus. A God who had come down to Earth. He was the God whom humanity had forgotten because the forces of the human body were evolving toward freedom. He appeared in a new form so that he could be seen and so that history could now speak of him as of an earthly being. The God who had only been known by human souls in the spiritual world descended and walked in Palestine. He consecrated the Earth through the fact that he entered an earthly body. For this reason the great question for those souls educated according to the culture of that age was this: What path had Christ taken in order to come to Jesus?

In the earliest times of Christianity the question concerning Christ was purely spiritual. The earthly biography of Jesus was not an object of research. The object of research was Christ and how he had descended from heaven. They looked up to suprasensory worlds, saw the descent of Christ to the Earth, and asked themselves: How has this supraearthly being become an earthly being? For this reason it was possible for the simple people who surrounded Christ as disciples to speak with him as a spirit also after his death. The most important part of what he could say after his death is preserved in only a few fragments. But spiritual science can find out what Christ said to those who were nearest to him after his death when he appeared to them in his purely spiritual form.

He spoke to them as the great healer, as the *Therapeut*, the comforter who knew the secret, the secret that human beings had once had a memory of him because they had been together with him in suprasensory worlds in their pre-earthly existence. Now he could say to them on Earth: Earlier I gave you the ability to remember your suprasensory, pre-earthly existence. Now, if you take me into your souls, if you take me into your hearts, I give you the power to go through the gate of death with consciousness of immortality. And you will no longer recognize the Father alone—*Ex deo nascimur*. You will feel the Son as the one with whom you can die and yet remain alive—*In Christo morimur*.

What Christ taught those who were near him after his bodily death was not, of course, expressed in the words I just used, but the meaning was the same. Primeval human beings had not known death, for from the moment they awakened to consciousness, they were aware of the soul that lived within. They knew about what lived in the soul and could not die. They could see people dying around them but this dying was a mere appearance, an illusion, among the facts surrounding them. They did not feel it as death. Only as The Mystery of Golgotha approached did human beings begin to feel the fact of dying. By then their soul life had become so much bound up with the life of the body that they could feel doubt concerning how the soul could continue to live when the body decays. In more ancient times no such question could have arisen because human beings knew the soul.

Christ now came as the one who said: I will live with you on the Earth so that you can have the power to awaken your soul with a new inner impulse. Your soul will be alive when you carry it through death. This is what Paul did not at first understand. He only understood it when access to suprasensory worlds was opened to him and he received living impressions of Jesus Christ here on the Earth. Pauline Christianity is less and less valued today for this reason—that it claims that Christ can be seen as coming from supraearthly worlds and uniting his supraearthly power with earthly humanity.

Thus, in the evolution of humanity, in human consciousness, the "out of God (that is, out of the Father God) we are born" was supplemented by the words of comfort, of life, and of power: "In Christ we die"—that is, We live in him.

We will best be able to place before our souls what humanity has become through The Mystery of Golgotha if I now describe, from the point of view of a present-day initiate, the evolution of humanity in the present and how we must hope for human beings to evolve in the future. I have already attempted to place before your souls the point of view of the ancient initiates, the point of view of the initiates at the time of The Mystery of Golgotha. Now I would like to try to describe the point of view of of present day initiates, those who approach life with more than mere knowledge of outer nature, those in whom deeper powers of knowledge have awakened. These are powers we can awaken in the soul through means given by spiritual literature.

When modern initiates acquire the scientific knowledge that is the triumph of our time—the glory in which so many people feel so comfortable (a comfort subtly enjoyed even by a certain higher consciousness)—they feel they are in a tragic situation. When modern initiates unite their souls with forms of knowledge especially useful and valuable in the world today, they experience a kind of dying. The more modern initiates (in whose souls the world of supraearthly spheres has been resurrected) are permeated by what the modern world calls science, the more they feel their souls dying. For modern initiates, the sciences are the soul's grave. The soul feels itself living together with death when it acquires world knowledge in the form of modern science. Sometimes such initiates feel this dying deeply and intensively. They then seek the reason they always die by knowing things in the modern sense, why they experience something like the odor of a corpse, just when they rise to the heights of modern scientific knowledge, the greatness of which initiates can truly appreciate, although such knowledge brings a premonition of death.

Then, from the initiates' knowledge of the suprasensory world, they say something to themselves that I would like to express through a picture. We live a life that is soul-spiritual before we come down to the Earth. What we experience in its full reality in the spiritual world during our pre-earthly existence we now experience on the Earth in our souls as mere ideas, concepts, and mental pictures. These are in our souls. But how do they live in our souls?

Let's look at human beings as we exist in the life between birth and death. We are fully alive, filled with living flesh and blood; we say that we are alive. Then we step across the threshold of death. Only a corpse remains of the physical human being, a corpse that is then given over to the elements of the Earth. We look at the physically dead human being; we have the corpse in front of us, the remains of the living, blood permeated human being. The human being is physically dead.

With the vision of initiation we now look back into our own souls. We look at our thoughts in the life between birth and death, at the thoughts arising from modern wisdom and science. And we recognize that just as the corpse of a human being is related to a fully alive human being, so too, our thoughts, the ones we revere as the highest riches knowledge of external nature

The Mystery of Golgotha

can bring us, are merely the corpse of what we were before we descended to the Earth. That is what initiates can experience. In their thoughts they do not experience their real life but the corpse of their soul. That is a fact. This is not said from any sentimentality; rather, it is what comes before the soul today with all intensity just when the soul is actively seeking knowledge with energy. This is not something that sentimental, mystical dreamers would say to themselves from some dark and mystic depths of their own being.

Those who walk through the gates of initiation today discovers these thoughts in their souls, thoughts that, precisely because they are *not* living, can make living freedom possible. These thoughts, which are the whole basis of human freedom, do not coerce us, precisely because they are dead, because they are not alive. Human beings today can become free because they work not with living but with dead thoughts. Dead thoughts can be grasped by us and used for freedom; but they are also experienced as a tragedy, as the corpse of the soul. Before the soul descended into the earthly world, everything that is a corpse today was full of life and movement. The beings of the higher hierarchies standing above us in the spiritual, suprasensory worlds moved between the souls of human beings who had already passed through death and now lived in the spiritual world or had not yet descended to Earth. Elemental beings who underlie all nature were also moving within this sphere. There everything in the soul was alive. Here the thoughts in our soul are the heritage from spiritual worlds and these thoughts are dead.

However, if as modern initiates we fill ourselves with Christ, who makes his life manifest in The Mystery of Golgotha, if we understand Paul's words, "Not I, but Christ in me," in their deepest sense, then Christ will also lead us through this death; then we can penetrate nature with our thoughts. Christ walks with us spiritually and he sinks our thoughts into the grave of the Earth. In as much as we usually have dead thoughts nature becomes a grave for us. Yet, if, with these dead thoughts, accompanied by Christ in the sense of the words, "Not I, but Christ in me," we approach the minerals, the animals, the world of stars, clouds, mountains, and streams, then we experience in modern initiation—if for example we immerse ourselves in quartz crystal—that thought arises from nature, from the quartz crystal as a living thought. As from the tomb of the mineral world, thought is raised up again as a living thought. The mineral world allows the spirit to resurrect in us. And just as Christ leads us everywhere through the plant world of nature, here too, where otherwise only dead thoughts would be found, living thoughts arise.

We would feel sick and unhealthy if we were to approach nature, looking up into the world of stars, with only the calculating vision of the astronomers, and if we then allowed these dead thoughts to sink into the world; we would feel sick and the sickness would be unto death. But if we let Christ accompany us, if we carry our dead thoughts in the presence of Christ into the world of stars, into the world of the Sun, of the Moon, of the clouds, mountains, rivers, minerals, plants, and animals, into the whole physical human world, then in our vision of nature everything comes alive. As if from a grave, from all beings in nature, the living spirit, the Holy Spirit arises, the one who heals and awakens us from death.

We must regain this in a spiritual knowledge, in a new knowledge of initiation. Then we will understand The Mystery of Golgotha as the meaning of the entire Earth existence; we will know that we need Christ to lead us to knowledge of nature now when human freedom is being developed through dead thoughts. We will know how Christ joined not only his own destiny to the Earth with his death in The Mystery of Golgotha, but, furthermore, how he gave to the Earth the great freedom of Pentecost when he promised earthly humanity the living spirit—the spirit who, with his help, can arise from everything on the Earth. Our knowledge remains dead, remains a sin even, if we have not been awakened by Christ so that from all nature, from all existence in the cosmos, the spirit speaks to us, the living spirit.

The idea of the Trinity of the Father God, of the Son God, and God of the Holy Spirit is not a cleverly thought-out formula. It is something deeply united with the entire evolution of the cosmos. When we bring Christ himself as the Resurrected One to life within us, then our knowledge of the Trinity is not dead but alive, for Christ is the bringer of the Holy Spirit.

We understand it is like a sickness to be unable to see the divine from which we are born. Human beings must be secretly sick if they are atheists. They are healthy only if their physical nature is constituted so that they can say, "From God I am born!" as the summation of how they feel within their own being. It is a blow of destiny when, in earthly life, people do not find Christ, the one who can lead them through death at the end of their Earth life, through death to knowledge.

If we feel *In Christo morimur*, we also feel what can approach us through the presence and guidance of Christ. We feel how the Spirit resurrects again from all things, even in this lifetime. We again feel ourselves to be alive in this earthly life. We look through the gate of death, through which Christ leads us; we look at the life that lies on the other side of death and know now why Christ sent the Holy Spirit—because we can unite with this Holy Spirit already here on Earth if we let ourselves be led by Christ. Then we can say with certainty that we die in Christ when we walk through the gate of death.

Our experience of nature on Earth with our natural scientific knowledge points significantly to the future. What otherwise would be dead science is resurrected through the living Spirit. For this reason, if we have understood the saying "From the Father are we born; in Christ we die," then when the death of knowledge is replaced by the real death that takes away our body, then in looking through the gate of death we can also say: In the Holy Spirit we shall be awakened again. *Per spiritum scanctum reviviscimus.*

4

THE OTHER SIDE OF HUMAN EXISTENCE

London, August 30, 1922

Since we can come together so seldom and would like to include as much as possible in these lectures, it could easily happen that too much is included. Nevertheless, today, from a certain point of view, I would still like to try to characterize for you what could be called the other side of human existence on Earth. I would then like to relate that to the significance of a deeper spiritual knowledge of our time.

How much do we finally know about our existence if we use only our senses and the intellect bound up with those senses as our source of knowledge? Ordinary sense-consciousness only allows us to spend the waking part of our existence in full consciousness. The spiritual powers that lead the world did not add the sleeping state to human existence for nothing. From falling asleep to waking up a very great deal happens to the human being. Indeed, most of what the spirit has to effect through human beings in earthly existence is actually achieved during the sleep state.

During the waking state, all that can occur on Earth is what we can undertake with ourselves and the things around us. But what higher, spiritual beings undertake with the human soul in human evolution, in order to bring the soul to complete development within earthly existence—this happens during the sleep state. We should not lose sight of the fact that modern initiation knowledge can look closely at the significance of the events that occur when the human being is asleep. Of course, these events occur not only for initiates but for all people; the development of all human beings depends upon them. The initiate can only draw attention to these sleep state events. However, every human being who gives any thought at all to the meaning of Earth existence should increasingly feel and sense the significance of what occurs while he sleeps.

Today I would simply like to describe all that plays into the sleeping state of the human being. As you know, when a person falls asleep we characterize what happens externally by saying that the astral body and the "I" are loosened from the physical and etheric bodies. The "I" and the astral body are then in the spiritual world; they no longer permeate the physical and etheric bodies as they did in the state between waking and falling asleep. When we look at what happens with human beings in the sleeping state our attention is drawn to the various ways they are connected to the Earth during waking.

To begin with, we are connected to the Earth through our senses—we perceive and know the appearances of the various kingdoms of nature. However, we are also connected with the Earth through what we do unconsciously while awake. For example, we breathe—for the most part, unconsciously—and the entire Earth, if I may put it this way, plays into the air we breathe. Innumerable substances dispersed in a very fine state are present in the air we breathe. Precisely because they are in this finely dispersed state they have an extraordinarily significant effect when inhaled into the human organism. What enters human beings when they perceive through the senses enters consciously. However a great deal also enters human beings unconsciously when we are awake. This unconscious element has more substance than what enters through the abstract, ideal state of perceiving and thinking. The world around us enters in a more substantial form through our breathing.

If you would only consider just how dependent the human organism is upon everything that it takes in with the various substances of earthly nourishment, then you would be able to acknowledge that there is much that affects us in our waking state. But this fact is of less interest to us today. We are much more concerned with what is working on the human being in a sleeping state. The point here is this: Just as we see external earthly substances connected with us during our waking state, so, too, when we enter the sleeping state, we enter into a certain connection with the entire cosmos.

That is not to say that we should imagine a human being taking on the magnitude of the cosmos every night with his or her astral body—that would be an exaggeration—but we do grow into the cosmos every night. Just as we are connected here on Earth during the day with the plants, the minerals, and the air, so too we are connected during the night with the movements of the planets and with the constellations of the fixed stars. From our falling asleep until our waking the sky full of stars becomes our world just as the Earth is our world in the waking state.

Now, to begin with, we can distinguish various spheres through which we pass between falling asleep and waking. The first sphere we pass through is that in which the human "I" and the human astral body—that is, the human soul when asleep—feels itself connected with the movements of the planets. When waking in the morning and, as it were, having slipped into our physical body we can say that we have in us our lungs, our heart, our liver, our brain. Likewise when we enter the sleep state we must say that in the first sphere with which we come into contact after falling asleep—which is also the sphere we are again in contact with just before awakening—in this sphere we have within us the forces of planetary movement.

It is not that we take the entire movements of the planets into ourselves every night. But what we carry within us as an image or copy is a small picture, in which the movements of the planets are actually copied, reflected. And this is different with every human being. We can say that, when falling asleep, every human being experiences the movements of the planets. Everything that goes on as movement "out there" in the space of the universe between the planets is experienced inwardly in a kind of globe of planets in the astral body. That is the human being's first experience after falling asleep.

Do not ask, my dear friends, what this has to do with you. Do not say that you do not perceive this. You may not see it with your eyes nor hear it with your ears. But in the moment you fall asleep, at that moment, that part of your astral body that during waking permeates and is a part of your heart—that part becomes an eye. We see with this organ, which I will call a "heart-eye." When we enter the sleep state this organ begins to perceive what is happening in the way I have just described. This heart-eye really does perceive what the human being experiences there—even if the perception is, for present-day humanity, very dim and obscure.

What we experience there is perceived by this heart-eye in such a way that, in the time after falling asleep when the physical and etheric bodies are lying there in bed, this heart-eye looks back at us. The "I" and the astral body look back at the physical and etheric bodies with the heart-eye. What the "I" and the astral body experience in their body inwardly as a picture of the movements of the planets, radiates back to the heart eye from their own etheric body. The "I" and the astral body see the mirror image of the planetary movement coming out of their own etheric body.

The Other Side of Human Existence

Upon awakening, because of the way the human being is presently constituted, we immediately forget the dim consciousness provided by our heart-eye during the night. This consciousness is dim and, at the most, can only be found echoing in certain dreams; in their inner flexibility these dreams still have something of the planetary movements. As we approach wakefulness, images from our lives settle into these dreams that, fundamentally speaking, are actually dependent upon the movements of the planets. The images enter at this point because the astral body is being submerged into the etheric body, which preserves our memories of earthly life.

The following is a specific example: You wake up in the morning; you have once again gone through the spheres of planetary movement. Let us say you have experienced there a special relationship between Jupiter and Venus because such an event is connected with your destiny, your karma. This could happen. You could have experienced a special relationship between Jupiter and Venus. If you could lift what was experienced there between Jupiter and Venus into the light of your day consciousness, then much concerning your human abilities would be clear to you. For those abilities have come from the cosmos, not from the Earth. How you are related to the cosmos determines how you are gifted, how you are good, or at least how you are inclined to good or to evil. You would be able to see what Jupiter and Venus discussed with one another, and what you perceived with your heart-eye. (I could just as well say heart-ear, for it is hard to distinguish such things.) But this is all forgotten because it has been perceived so very dimly. As this exchange between Jupiter and Venus continues within you it causes corresponding movements in your astral body and something else, from your etheric body, mixes in—for example, what you experienced around noon when you were seventeen, or when you were twenty-five years old, say, in Oxford or Manchester or anywhere. Such earthly images are mixed with the cosmic experiences. The pictures in dreams do have a certain significance; but the pictures are not what is of primary importance. They are, so to speak, the fabric woven to clothe cosmic events.

Concerning the experience that thus comes into existence for the perception of the heart, we can say that it is bound up with a certain anxiety. For almost everyone there are feelings of a spiritual kind of anxiety mixed in with this experience, especially when what was experienced cosmically shines back and echoes from the human etheric body. For example, this anxiety arises for the perception of the heart if what has been brought about through the special relationship between Jupiter and Venus radiates back with a ray—which would say a lot for your heart perception—radiates back from the human forehead, and if this ray is then mixed with the sound and light from another ray, say, from the region just below the heart. This perception of anxiety leads every soul not entirely hardened to such perceptions to actually say to itself in sleep: The mists of the cosmos have taken me into themselves. It really feels like you have become as thin as the mists of the world and are swimming like a cloud, just a part of cosmic fog, within the larger mists of the cosmos. This is the experience immediately after falling asleep.

Then out of this anxiety, out of this feeling of one's self as just another mist within the cosmic fog, something comes into the human soul that could be called devotion to the divine that is weaving through the world. Those are the two basic feelings that come over the human being in the first sphere after falling asleep: first that I am within the mists of the world, and then that I would like to rest in the bosom of God so as to be safe from dissolution in these mists. These feelings must be carried by the perception of the heart when we again awaken in the morning and enter into our physical and etheric bodies. If this experience were not carried over into life then all the substances we take into our bodies for nourishment the next day, or whatever else our metabolism may process—even if we starve, for then the substances are taken from our bodies—these substances would assume solely their earthly character and would thus bring about disorder in the whole human organism.

It is simply a fact that for the human waking condition the significance of sleep is enormous. In this epoch of Earth's development, humankind is still spared the task of having to carry the divine from sleep into waking. Because of the way human beings in the present age are constituted they could hardly muster the strength to carry these things in full consciousness from the other side of existence to this side of existence.

After the experiences connected with the planetary movements, the human being goes into the next sphere. In doing so we do not leave the first; it remains for the perception of the heart. The next sphere is much more complicated and is perceived with that part of the astral body that, during the day, during waking, permeates and is a part of the solar plexus, permeates and is a part of our entire limb system. The solar plexus and limb system of the human being, that part of the astral body that penetrates and permeates the solar plexus and the arms and legs—this part of the astral body perceives what happens in the night in the next sphere.

In the next sphere we feel the forces in our astral bodies that originate in the constellations of the zodiac. These forces come in two forms, the first consisting of those forces that come directly from the constellations of the zodiac, the other form arising when these forces from the zodiac pass through the Earth. It makes a very big difference whether the zodiacal signs are above or below the Earth.

In this sphere the human being perceives with what I would like to call "Sun perception" because that part of the astral body connected with the solar plexus and the limb system is involved in the perception. I would like to call this perceiving part of the astral body the "eye of the Sun" or the "Sun-eye." Through it we become aware of our entire relationship to the zodiac and the movements of the planets. In this sphere the picture is enlarged, we grow more into the picture of the cosmos.

This experience is again mirrored to us by our own physical and etheric bodies, which we are now looking at. What comes forth from our body every night is brought into connection with the entire cosmos, with the movements of the planets and the constellations of the fixed stars. The experience with the fixed stars may occur for some people half an hour after falling asleep, for some after a longer period and for others very shortly after falling asleep. We experience ourselves in all twelve constellations. The experiences with the fixed stars are extraordinarily complicated.

My dear friends, I believe you could have visited the most important regions of the Earth as a world traveler and still you would not have had the sum of experiences that your Sun-eye gathers for you from a single constellation of the zodiac. Because the people who lived in ancient times still had powerful dreamlike powers of clairvoyance and perceived, in a dreamlike way, much of what I have been describing, all of this was relatively less confusing to them. Today, a person's Sun-eye can hardly come to any kind of clarity—and we must come to clarity even if we forget it in the day. We can hardly come to any kind of clarity concerning what we experience in twelvefold complexity during the night unless we take into our hearts and minds what Christ wanted to become for the Earth through The Mystery of Golgotha. Simply having felt what it means for the life of the

Earth that Christ went through The Mystery of Golgotha, simply thinking about Christ in our ordinary life on Earth brings such a tinge, such a hue, into our astral body, by the indirect path through the physical and etheric bodies, that Christ can become our leader through the zodiac from falling asleep to waking.

Once again the human being wonders: Will I be lost in the multitude of stars and their activities? But if we can look back to thoughts, feelings, and will impulses turned toward Christ during our daytime waking state, then Christ becomes a leader who helps us to bring order into the complex and confusing events of this sphere.

Only when we observe the other side of life do we realize the full significance of Christ for the Earth life of humanity since The Mystery of Golgotha. In the present, ordinary civilization, there is actually no one else who understands what Christ must still become for the life of Earth. All these things, which have not yet been experienced by many people, are wrongly explained. Only when you know what I have just explained can you understand the various ways people who have not yet been touched by the Christ event bring their nightly experiences while asleep into waking day consciousness. When we have gone through the misty existence in the sleep state and entered the second sphere we stand before a complicated and confusing world. Only when Christ steps forward as a spiritual Sun and becomes our leader is complex confusion resolved into a kind of harmonious understanding.

This point is important because our karma appears, actually appears to our Sun-eye, the moment we step into this sphere of whirling confusion, this sphere of planetary movement and of the fixed star constellations of the zodiac. All human beings perceive their karma, but only in the sleeping state. The afterimage or afterglow of this perception slips into our waking state through our feelings.

Much of the condition of soul that we can find in ourselves—if, to some extent, we strive for self-knowledge—is a very dim echo of this zodiacal experience. People can receive strength for their daily lives because Christ appeared as the leader and led them from Aries through Taurus, Gemini, and so forth, and explained the world to them in the night. What we experience in this sphere is nothing less significant than this: Christ becomes our leader through the complex and confusing events in the zodiac; he stands there as the being who leads us, who leads us from constellation to constellation, in order for us to take into ourselves, in an orderly fashion, the spiritual forces that we once again need—and they are, indeed, ordered—for our waking life.

Fundamentally, this is what human beings experience every night between falling asleep and waking. We experience this because we are related to the cosmos as a soul and spirit. Just as we are related to the Earth through our etheric and physical bodies, we are also related to the cosmos with our soul, spirit, and astral bodies. When human beings have separated from their physical and etheric bodies and grown out into the cosmic world, they then feels inwardly a strong kinship to the world they are entering. We feel this kinship in our experience of the pictures reflected back to us from what has been left lying in bed. We feels a strong tendency to move out beyond the zodiac with our inner life, but we cannot do this between birth and death because another element mixes into all these experiences during the time we are asleep, one that, compared to what comes from the planets and fixed stars, has an entirely different nature. This is the Moon element.

During the night the element of the Moon, even during the new Moon, tinges to a certain extent the entire cosmos with a special something that is like a substance. This tinging is also experienced by us. But we experience it in such a way that these

The Other Side of Human Existence

Moon forces hold us back within the world of the zodiac and lead us once again to waking. With a dimly conscious awareness we already experience this Moon element in the first sphere. But during the second sphere we experience the secrets of birth and death in an especially powerful way. With an organ lying even deeper than the heart-eye and the Sun-eye, with an organ that is, so to speak, apportioned to the whole human being, we actually experience every night how our soul-spirit being descends—that is, has descended—from the world of soul and spirit and has entered into physical existence through birth; and we experience how the body gradually goes over into death. We are actually always dying. In every moment we only subdue death until it actually occurs as a single event. But the moment we experience how the soul, so to speak, goes through Earthly nature, bodily nature, in this same moment we also experience—and through the very same forces—our connection with the rest of humanity.

You have to remember this: Not even the most insignificant encounter, insignificant relationship—or even the most decisive—is without a connection to our total destiny, to the total karma of the human being. All our involvement with other human beings, all human relationships, which have, of course, an intimate connection with the mystery of birth and death, appear, I would like to say, before our spiritual eye at this point during the second sphere. This comprehension of karma happens whether the souls with whom we have ever had a connection in past lives, or with whom we now, in this Earth life, have a relationship, are presently in the spiritual world or are on the Earth. We feel ourselves at this point to be in touch with and living within our total life destiny.

This experience is connected with the fact that all the other forces, those of the planets and the fixed stars, want to draw us out into the cosmos while the Moon wants to put us again into the world of people, basically tearing us out of the cosmos. The Moon has forces that are actually opposed to the forces of the Sun as well as the forces of the stars. It constitutes our kinship to the Earth. For this reason every night, in a certain sense, it brings us back from the experiences of the zodiac into the planetary experiences and once again into earthly experiences, in that we are brought back into the physical body of a human being. From a certain point of view this is the difference between sleeping and dying: When a human being merely falls asleep he or she maintains a strong connection to these Moon forces. Every night, in a certain sense, these Moon forces also point out to us again the meaning of our life on Earth. But this can only be the case because we receive everything reflected back from the etheric body.

In death we pull the etheric body out of the physical body; the backward view of memories from the last life on Earth then appears. For a short while, a few days, the etheric body permeates the cloud about which I have spoken. As I said, every night we experience ourselves as a cloud, as a cloud of mists in a world of fog. But this cloud of mists that we ourselves are, this cloud is without our etheric body during the night. When we die the cloud is, to begin with, in the first days after our death, with our etheric body. Then the etheric body gradually dissolves into the cosmos and our memory disappears. And now, in contrast to what we had earlier when our experience of the stars was only radiated back from the human being, who remained lying in bed, now, after death, we have an immediate, inner experience of the movements of the planets and the fixed star constellations.

If you read my book *Theosophy*[1] you will find, described from a certain point of view, what these experiences after death consist of. I describe what appears as if surrounding the human being between death and a new birth. But just as the world would have no color if there were no eyes in your body, no sounds if you were without ears, just as you could not breathe without lungs and a heart, so too, after death you would not be able to perceive what I have described as the soul world and spirit land, your environment in the spiritual world, unless you had Mercury, Venus, Mars, Jupiter, Aries, Taurus, Gemini, and so forth. That is then your organism: with your cosmic organism you experience all of this. The Moon can no longer bring you back because it could only bring you back to an etheric body; but your etheric body has been dissolved into the cosmos.

As I described the process in *Theosophy*, there is still so much left of the power bequeathed to the human being by the Moon that after death we must remain a while in the soul world. We keep looking at the Earth intently, until we go over into what I described as spirit land. There we experience ourselves as being beyond the zodiac, beyond the realm of the fixed stars. In this way we live through the time between death and a new birth. I could describe the details of this entry into, and life within, the spiritual world—the entry made every night. But the concepts I use for this description must not be pushed too far; these things can hardly be expressed with earthly concepts. Nevertheless, I can describe it to you as follows.

Picture a meadow and picture flowers in this meadow; from every blossom in the meadow and on the trees, a kind of spiral goes forth unwinding upward into cosmic space. The spirals contain the forces through which the cosmos regulates and effects the growth of plants on the Earth. For plants grow not only out of their seeds; plants grow out of the cosmic, helical forces that surround the Earth. These forces are also present in winter, also in the desert, and also when there are no plants present. In order to enter into the movements of the planets every night we must use these helical forces as a ladder. Using the ladder-like quality of the spiraling forces of the plants we climb up into the movements of the planetary world. With the force that the plant uses to grow upward, a force coming forth from its roots (you see, it has to apply a force in order to grow upwards) with this force the human being is carried into the second sphere that I described. When it comes to those experiences I have described for you—when we are beset by a certain anxiety and say: I am a figure of mists in the universal cosmic fog, I must rest in the bosom of God—when we consider these experiences with respect to conditions on the Earth, then, again, the soul can say to itself: I rest in all of what lays like a cosmic blessing over a field of grain when it blossoms, which lays over a meadow when it blossoms. Everything that sinks down to the plants lives and expresses itself in the spiraling lines of force, is, fundamentally speaking, the bosom of God, the bosom of God enlivened and active within itself. Therein the human being feels embedded in every period of sleep.

The Moon leads us back again to our animal nature while the forces of plants constantly strive to carry us further out into the universe. In this way we are connected with the cosmos. In this way the cosmos works between our falling asleep and our waking. And the heart-eye, Sun-eye, and human eye go through the night feeling things in a way similar to the way, say, that we experience any kind of relationship to another human being. But we are not told this, neither do we think this out by ourselves, but rather the plants tell us this, the plants, which give us a ladder to climb up into the planetary world where we are then forced out into the world of the zodiac.

One could have an experience like this: I have a relationship to a particular person; the lilies tell me, the roses tell me, because the forces of the roses, the forces of the lilies, the forces of the tulips have driven me precisely to this place. The entire

The Other Side of Human Existence

Earth becomes a kind of "book of life" that enlightens us about the human world, the world in which we live, the world of human souls.

People of various ages and epochs have had these experiences in different ways. When you look at ancient India you see that those wanting to discover something through the sleeping state, through a relationship with the world of the stars, wanted information only from those fixed stars and constellations that happened to be above the Earth at any given time. They never wanted connections to the constellations below, the constellations whose forces had to go through the Earth. Just take a look at the Buddha posture or at the posture of any sages whatsoever from the East who strive for spiritual wisdom through exercises. Consider how they cross their legs, one over the other, and sit on them. They assume this posture because they want only the upper body and what is connected to the stars above to become active within. They do not want what also works through them, through the Sun-eye, and through the limb system to become inwardly active. They want the forces of the limb system more or less excluded. Therefore, you can see, in the position of all Eastern students striving for wisdom, how they want to develop a relationship only to what is above the Earth. They want to develop only the connections that lead to knowledge in the soul realm.

The world would have remained incomplete if this had remained the only kind of search for knowledge—if, to acquire knowledge, we had been restricted to the Buddha posture alone. Even during the Greek age, people had to enter a relationship with the forces encountered when they developed in the direction of the constellations that, at any given time, are below the Earth. This tendency is hinted at in a wonderfully intimate way in Greek tales. We are always told of a kind of initiation in Greek tales. When it is said that certain Greek heroes descended into the underworld, that they experienced initiation, it means that they became acquainted with the forces that work through the Earth. They came to know the chthonic powers.

Every age has a special task. To teach other people, the Eastern initiate learned primarily about what could be found before birth—actually, before conception—that is, what exists in the soul-spiritual realms that human beings live through before descending to the earthly world. What approaches us in such a magnificent way in Eastern writings and the Eastern worldview comes to us because people back then could look into the life human beings led before they descended to the Earth.

In Greece people began to know the forces that depended upon the Earth itself: Uranus and Gaia. Gaia, the Earth, stands at the beginning of Greek cosmology. The Greek always sought to find out about, to know, the mysteries of the Earth itself, mysteries that were, of course, also cosmic mysteries that worked through the Earth. The Greeks wanted to know about the mysteries of the underworld. In this way the Greeks developed a proper cosmology.

Consider how little knowledge of history (as we call it) the Greeks had. Yet the Eastern person never had any at all. The Greeks were far more interested in what was going on when the Earth was being formed in the cosmos and then later when the inner powers of the Earth, the Titanic forces, fought against other powers. The Greeks pointed to these gigantic, powerful spiritual forces that form the foundation for earthly conditions and in which humanity is so entangled. It is incumbent upon us in the new age to understand history and be able to point out that humanity has come out of an old, dreamlike clairvoyant condition, that we have now arrived at an intellectually colored consciousness that is merely tinged with the mythical. We must now work our way out of this consciousness and once again into a seeing into the spiritual world.

The present epoch marks the transition to a conscious experience of the spiritual world that can only be achieved with effort. For this purpose we must, above all, look at history. We have, therefore, in our anthroposophical movement, again and again reviewed the various historical epochs from our time all the way back to the time when human beings still received knowledge from higher, supraearthly beings. We have followed the historical development of humanity.

The external knowledge of our time views this historical human development in a completely abstract way. What abstract lines are drawn when people today develop knowledge of history! Ancient peoples followed a history still clothed in mythos, a history that included nature and its events. We can no longer do that. But people have not yet acquired a faculty that would lead them to ask: What was it like when the first human beings received wisdom from higher beings? And what was it like as that wisdom gradually faded away? What was it like when a god descended to incarnate in a human body through The Mystery of Golgotha, to fulfill a grand, cosmic mission with the Earth, so that the Earth could receive its meaning?

The whole of nineteenth and twentieth century theology suffers from the inability to understand the spiritual significance of Christ. You see, modern initiation science must bring this understanding. There must be a modern science of initiation that can penetrate once again into the spiritual world, that can speak once again about birth and death, about life between birth and death and life between death and a new birth, and about the life of the human soul in sleep just as we here today have spoken to one another. Once again it must be possible for humankind to know about this spiritual, other side of existence. All of humanity's future progress will be possible only if human beings also become acquainted with this other side of existence.

Once people turned to the upper worlds alone for their knowledge. This can easily be observed in the posture of the Buddha. Later people came to their cosmology by reading it out of the development of the Earth; they were initiated in the Greek chthonic mysteries, as passages in the Greek myths recount again and again. Now that the secrets of heaven and the secrets of Earth have been studied in the old science of initiation we need a *modern* science of initiation that can move back and forth between heaven and Earth, that can ask heaven when it wants to know something about Earth and that can ask the Earth when it wants to know something about heaven.

If I may say so in all modesty, this is how the questions are posed and given preliminary answers in my book *An Outline of Esoteric Science.*[2] The attempt is made there to describe what modern human beings need, just as ancient Eastern humanity needed the mysteries of heaven and the Greeks needed the mysteries of the Earth. In our age we should observe how things stand with this modern initiation and its relationship to modern humanity.

To characterize briefly the tasks that form the foundation of modern initiation I will say something now that I was already able to say to a few of you in Oxford during these days of my visit to England—that is, I would like to begin by pointing out that, whereas it was important for the most ancient initiates to look up into the spiritual world from which human beings descended when they clothed themselves in an earthly body, and whereas for later initiates such things as I characterized by pointing to Greek portrayals of a descent into the underworld were important, it is the obligation of *modern* initiation, as I have said, to seek as knowledge the rhythmic relationship of Heaven and Earth.

The Other Side of Human Existence

This can be achieved only by considering the following. Certainly, we must know Heaven, and certainly we must know the Earth. But then we must also look at human beings, in whom, among all the beings around us, Heaven and Earth work together to create a unity. We must look at the human being—that is, with our Sun-eye, our heart-eye, with the entire human eye. The human being! Humanity contains infinitely more secrets than the worlds we can perceive with our outer organs of perception and that we can explain with an intellect bound to the senses. The task of present-day initiation knowledge is to come to know the human being spiritually. I would like to say that initiation science wants to come to know everything for this reason: to understand the human being through knowledge of the whole world, through knowledge of the whole cosmos.

Now compare the situation of the present-day initiate with the situation of the ancient initiate. Because of all the abilities that existed in the soul of ancient humanity the initiate then could awaken memories of the time before the descent into an earthly body. For this reason initiation for the ancient was an awakening of cosmic memories. Then, for the Greeks, initiation meant looking into nature. Modern initiates are concerned to know the human being directly as a spiritual being. Now we must acquire the ability to set ourselves free from the grasp of Earth, from the ties connecting us with the world. I would like to repeat an example that I have just recently mentioned.

Achieving a relationship to the souls who have passed through the gate of death, who have left the Earth, either recently or long ago, is one of the most difficult tasks of initiation knowledge. However, it *is* possible to achieve such a relationship by awakening forces that lie deeper in the soul. Here we must understand clearly, however, that we have to accustom ourselves, through exercises, to the language we must speak with the dead. This language is, I would like to say, in a certain sense, a child of human language. But we would go completely astray if we thought that this human language here could help us to cultivate communication with the dead.

The first thing we become aware of is that the dead are only able to understand for a short time what lives as nouns in the language of Earth. What is expressed as a thing, a closed off thing, the characterization of a noun, is no longer present in the language of the dead. In the language of the dead everything is related to activity and movement. For this reason we find that some time after we have passed through the gate of death, we have a real feeling only for verbs. To communicate with the dead we must sometimes direct a question to them by formulating it in such a way that it is understandable to them. Then, if we know how to pay attention, the answer comes after a while. Usually several nights must pass before the deceased person can give us an answer to our questions.

However, we must first find our way into the language of the deceased. Finally the language appears for us, one the dead actually have, the language the deceased has had to live into after death, distancing themselves from the Earth with their whole soul life. We find our way into a language that is not at all formed according to earthly conditions, but is rather a language arising from feelings, from the heart. It is a kind of language of the heart. Here, language is formed in the way vowels or feeling sounds are formed in human language. For example, when we are amazed we say "Ah!" or when we want to lead ourselves back to ourselves we speak the "ee" sound. Only in such instances do the sounds and sound combinations receive their due, their real meaning. And beginning with such instances language becomes something that no longer sounds bound up to the speech organ. It is transformed into what I have just described, a language of the heart. When we have learned this transformed language, the forces that rise from the flowers give us information about humankind and we ourselves begin to speak with what comes from the flowers. When we enter into the tulip blossom with our soul forces we express, in the Imagination of the tulip, what is expressed here on the Earth in the formation of words. We grow again into the spiritual aspect of everything.

From the example of language, just characterized, you see that human beings grow into entirely different conditions of existence once they have gone through the gate of death. You see, we really know very little about human beings if we know only their external side; the modern science of initiation must know the other side. This begins with language. Even the human body, as it is described if you read the relevant literature, becomes something else for us. The body becomes a world in itself when we grow into the science of initiation.

Whereas initiates of ancient times reawakened an ability in people that had been lost, and whereas they brought to memory what they had experienced before descending to the Earth, initiate today must do something entirely new, something that represents progress in the human being, that will still have significance for us when humanity itself will one day have left the Earth, indeed, when the Earth is no longer even present in the cosmos. This is the task of modern initiation science. Modern initiation science must speak from this strength.

As you know, from time to time the science of initiation enters into the spiritual development of the Earth. This has happened again and again. The initiation science we need actually sees only a beginning in the assumptions of contemporary science. This initiation science will be increasingly contested. You will need strength to get through all that stands against modern initiation. Before modern initiation, which is a conversation with suprasensory powers, actually first received its proper power in the last third of the nineteenth century, the adversarial powers were already at work to bring about a condition of human culture and civilization, in many ways an unconscious condition, which actually amounts to a complete extermination of modern initiation.

Consider how popular it has become to respond to everything that appears in the world as knowledge by saying, "This is *my* point of view." People say this without having gone through any kind of development. People are all supposed to make their own point of view count from the location where they just happen to be standing at the moment they speak. Moreover, people are offended, even angry, when a higher knowledge is mentioned, one that can be acquired only through the work of self-development.

When the possibility of achieving a modern initiation appeared, primarily in the last third of the nineteenth century, adversary powers were already at work. Above all they wanted to bring about a great leveling of people, also in the spiritual realm. There are many people I could mention through whom these enemies of modern initiation have worked.

My dear friends, you must believe that the words I must speak from the spirit of this initiation science must also sound the way they do from the perspective of ordinary conditions here on the Earth. If I try to make clear to you how the sounds of human language become different when language is to be used in the presence of the beings of the spiritual world, then you will not misunderstand me when I say that I myself will never misunderstand the great significance, spoken from the merely earthly point of view, of someone like Rousseau. And if I speak from the merely earthly standpoint, I will set out with all élan to praise and speak well of Rousseau, just as others speak of him.[3] But if I should rise to an attempt to clothe in earthly words what initiation knowledge says concerning Rousseau, I would have to say that with his equalization, with his spiritual leveling, Rousseau represents the supreme babbler of modern civilization.

This is something that humanity cannot readily assimilate, that someone like Rousseau can be called a great spirit, a great personality, from the earthly point of view but—if we really want to get to know this person through the modern science of initiation (where we must know heaven and Earth and describe the rhythm between them from both sides)—must be called the supreme babbler from the point of view of initiation. Only the harmony of what resounds from the one side and from the other side leads to a true knowledge of the human being. This true knowledge of the human being must be built on the same wisdom on which the ancient initiates build: *Ex deo nascimur*. All remembering must by built upon what comes to meet us when we look out into the world where, as I have today described the process, we have unconsciously allowed Christ to become our leader. But we must bring him into our consciousness more and more. Then we can recognize what belongs to death in the world as standing under the leadership of Christ. Then we can recognize that we live into the dead world with Christ: *In Christo morimur*.

Finally, because we are submerged in the grave of the Earth and its life we experience with Christ the resurrection and the sending of the Spirit: *Per spiritum sanctum reviviscimus*.

Modern initiates must strive above all for this *Per spiritum sanctum reviviscimus*. If you consider this counsel and compare it with the modern attitude coming from science you will recognize that there will still be immense opposition, perhaps of a kind you cannot even imagine today, which will take the form of external actions and deeds that, above all, will have a tendency to make initiation science entirely impossible. What I would like to leave in your hearts, in your souls, when I speak in such an intimate circle of friends, is this: Through the descriptions given by modern initiation science, I would like to awaken strength so that a few people are actually present in the world who can find the proper place between what wants to come into the earthly world from spiritual worlds and what, from the direction of the earthly world, wants it to be impossible for spirituality to penetrate into the life of Earth.

This is what I have wanted to point out in such an intimate circle of friends. An opportunity had already been given to speak in a more exoteric lecture, such as, to my great satisfaction, we were able to have in Oxford. Since the opportunity was given to describe the exoteric side, so the esoteric side must also be handled in this smaller circle, it must also be described. I believe it would be good if you could get beyond the fact that there is much that sounds paradoxical when I speak out of spiritual worlds. It has to sound paradoxical because the language of spiritual worlds is so different from any earthly language. What should actually be expressed differently can only be brought into earthly language with a great exertion of force. Therefore, it should be understandable if some things are shocking when they appear unmediated as a simple description of spiritual worlds.

My dear friends, in addition to characterizing the fundamental intention that was behind today's lecture, I also want to express my deep satisfaction that I have been able to be here and speak to you in London. It is always gratifying. As I have already said, we are seldom together here. May what we can found in our hearts, in our souls, through such rare gatherings bring about a togetherness that should always be present among those who call themselves anthroposophists—a togetherness of hearts and souls extending over the whole world. Today's lecture has

The Other Side of Human Existence

been given with this goal in mind, that we use such brief times together as an inspiration for the greater togetherness that unites all our hearts and all our souls. And to document, as it were, this intention I would like to add the following words.

Speaking from this frame of mind, I would like to say: Let us remain together, my dear friends, even as we leave now to go in such widely separate directions.

NOTES

Part One

Lecture 1

1. Julian, the Apostate (332–363), Roman Emperor (361–363). Steiner is referring to his lecture of July 16, 1922 (GA213). Cf. Rudolf Steiner: *Occult History* (lect. 4), *Building Stones for an Understanding of The Mystery of Golgotha* (lect. 7), *World History in the Light of Anthroposophy* (lect. 6).
2. Ernst von Wildenbruch (1845–1909), German writer, author of historical dramas, novels, and verse.
3. St. Augustine, Bishop of Hippo (354–430). Early Latin church father. Exerted tremendous influence on later Christian thought. Cf. Rudolf Steiner: *Christianity as Mystical Fact*; and *Building Stones for an Understanding of the Mystery of Golgotha* (lect. 7).
4. Steiner is here referring to an essay by Günther Wachsmuth on Dionysius the Areopagite and the doctrine of the hierarchies that appeared in *Das Goetheanum*, July 23 and July 30, 1922.
5. Lecture of July 22, 1922 (GA213).
6. Lecture of July 16, 1922 (GA213).
7. *Heliand*, a poem in alliterative verse on the Gospels written between AD 825 and 835.
8. E.g., *Pelerinage de Charlemagne* (eleventh century), *Gran Conquista de Ultramar* (thirteenth century).
9. Charlemagne (724–814), King of France and Roman Emperor. The Untersberg is a mountain ridge, full of caves, near Salzburg, Austria. Frederick Barbarossa (Redbeard) or Frederick I (1123–1190), Holy Roman Emperor. Esteemed by Germans as one of their greatest kings.
10. Peers of Charlemagne's court.
11. Lohengrin, a knight of the Grail, son of Parsifal. Led by a swan to rescue Princess Elsa of Brabant, he then marries her. When she asks his name, in violation of her pledge, he must return to the Grail Castle without her. Tale ascribed to Wolfram von Eschenbach (c. 1285–90); basis for Richard Wagner's opera, *Lohengrin* (1847).
12. Henry I (c. 876–936), first German king from the House of Saxony, campaigned in Hungary in 933.
13. Martianus Minneus Felix, Latin author of the fourth to fifth centuries, author of *The Marriage of Philology and Mercury*, the encyclopaedic work in verse and prose that introduced the Seven Liberal Arts to the Middle Ages.

14. Johann Gregor Mendel. Augustinian priest and botanist, creator of Mendelian genetics. Mendel did his famous breeding experiments in the monastery garden in 1856. Results published 1866. Not widely recognized until after 1910.

Lecture 2

1. Johann Wolfgang von Goethe (1749–1832), German poet and thinker. Published *Metamorphosis of Plants* in 1790; in this book he shows the leaf as the primeval organ of the plant from which all other plant organs evolved.
2. Karl von Linné (Linnaeus) (1107–1778), Swedish naturalist, father of modern systematic botany.
3. Johann Gottlieb Fichte (1762–1814), German idealist philosopher. Important for the development of Anthroposophy. See Rudolf Steiner: *Truth and Science* and *The Riddle of Man*.
4. Paracelsus (1493–1541), Renaissance alchemist, doctor, and philosopher. Cf. Rudolf Steiner: *Mysticism at the Dawn of the Modern Age*, *The Origins of Modern Science* (lect. 8).

Lecture 3

1. John Scotus Eriugena (c. 810–877), Neoplatonizing Celtic Christian philosopher. Cf. Rudolf Steiner, *Riddles of Philosophy*, *Occult History*, *The Origins of Modern Science*.
2. Gottschalk of Orbais, Benedictine monk, also at Fulda. Caused great controversy with teachings on the predestination of the elect. Condemned for heresy by the Synod of Mainz (848).
3. Cf. St. Augustine, *City of God*, Books XII, XIII.
4. Ratramnus of Corbie (d. 868+), Theologian and controversialist.
5. Johann Christoph Friedrich von Schiller (1759–1805), German poet, dramatist, historian, and philosopher. Schiller's friendship with Goethe is celebrated. Strongly influenced by Kant, his idealism and hatred of tyranny were a powerful influence in modern German literature. Wrote *On the Aesthetic Education of Man* (1795).
6. Imanuel Kant (1724–1804), German philosopher of the Enlightenment. Published *Critique of Pure Reason* (1781).
7. Friedrich Wilhelm Nietzche (1844–1900), German philosopher and poet. Professor of classical philology, Basel (1869–1879). Known for denouncing religion, and for espousing the perfectibility of human beings through forcible self-assertion. Published *The Birth of Tragedy from the Spirit of Music* (1872).
8. Johann Wolfgang von Goethe, "Fairy Tale of the Green Snake and the Beautiful Lily" (Blauvelt, NY: SteinerBooks, 1979).
9. Friedrich Heinrich Jacobi (1743–1819), president of the Munich Academy. In opposition to the thinkers of the Enlightenment, he recognized only two types of people: Christian believers and those

who trusted their reason. Reason, Jacobi taught, is not the way to arrive at ultimate truth .
10. Schiller, *Votiftafeln: Mein Glaube*.

Lecture 4

1. Goethe was a member of the secret fraternal order of Free and Accepted Masons. Not restricted to stoneworkers, it retains much of the spirit and code of the medieval mason's guild.

Part Two

Lecture 1

1. Rudolf Steiner, *How to Know Higher Worlds: A Modern Path of Initiation* (Hudson, NY: Anthroposophic Press, 1994).

Lecture 2

1. Rudolf Steiner, *Theosophy: An Introduction to the Spiritual Processes in Human Life and in the Cosmos* (Hudson, NY: Anthroposophic Press, 1994).
2. Rudolf Steiner, *Intuitive Thinking as a Spiritual Path: A Philosophy of Freedom* (Hudson, NY: Anthroposophic Press, 1994).

Lecture 4

1. Rudolf Steiner, *Theosophy: An Introduction to the Suprasensory Knowledge of the World and the Destination of Man,* (Hudson, NY: Anthroposophic Press, 1986).
2. Rudolf Steiner, *An Outline of Esoteric Science* (Hudson, NY: Anthroposophic Press, 1997).
3. Jean Jacques Rousseau (1712–1778), French philosopher. Influential in shaping Romanticism. Contending that people are good by nature and corrupted by civilization, Rousseau advocated a social contract to uphold the sovereignty of the people as a whole.

www.ingramcontent.com/pod-product-compliance
Lightning Source LLC
Chambersburg PA
CBHW020903090426
42736CB00008B/482